# THE

# JOHANNINE

# LOGOS

by

Gordon H. Clark

Distributed by

## BAKER BOOK HOUSE
Grand Rapids, Michigan

1972

278

The Johannine Logos

International Library of Philosophy and Theology
BIBLICAL AND THEOLOGIAL STUDIES
Robert L. Reymond, Editor

Printed in the United States of America

## THE AUTHOR

Gordon H. Clark, professor of philosophy at Butler University, and, since 1945, head of that department, is a graduate of the University of Pennsylvania and earned his Ph.D. at that institution, continuing his graduate studies in the Sorbonne, Paris. Prior to his appointment at Butler University, Dr. Clark taught at the University of Pennsylvania and at Wheaton College.

Dr. Clark's major publications include: *Readings in Ethics* (with T. V. Smith), 1931; *Selections from Hellenistic Philosophy*, 1940; *A History of Philosophy* (with Martin, et al.), 1941; *A Christian Philosophy of Education*, 1946; *A Christian View of Men and Things*, 1952; *What Presbyterians Believe*, 1956; *Thales to Dewey*, 1956; and *Dewey* (Modern Thinkers Series), 1960.

# CONTENTS

Chapter 1
   Introduction ............................... 7

Chapter 2
   The Prologue .............................. 15

Chapter 3
   Logos and Rheemata ....................... 38

Chapter 4
   Truth ..................................... 47

Chapter 5
   Saving Faith .............................. 69

# Chapter I
## INTRODUCTION

The Gospel of John is the most hated book of the Bible, and the most beloved—for the same reason, namely, that it was written that you might believe that Jesus is the Christ, the Son of God, and that believing you might have life through his name. If the contents of a book were not important, it could not be very much hated or very much beloved. The contents of this Gospel are extremely important. Therefore it abounds with points suitable for discussion and controversy. The point for discussion here, as the title indicates, is the Johannine Logos. As a most important point it has been discussed in many volumes. They usually restrict themselves to the first few verses of the first chapter and ignore, for a reason but an inadequate reason, how John used the *Logos* in the remainder of the Gospel. This additional material will not be ignored here.

In studies on John or on the New Testament as a whole, it is customary to begin with what is called *Introduction*. The word is used in a more technical sense than is found in most other subjects. College curricula have courses called Introduction to Psychology, Introduction to Botany, Introductory Logic, and so on. These courses give their students the first and easiest parts of the subjects indicated. But an Introduction to the Gospel of John is not very easy, and it is so far from summarizing the main contents of the book that it gives its readers hardly any notion of what the Gospel is all about. Introduction discusses questions such as authorship and date. It asks, Was the author a disciple who ate the last Passover with Jesus and participated in the first Lord's Supper, John, the son of Zebedee? Or was he someone else of the same name? Or perhaps the author was an unknown person in the late second or early third century who, with a good imagination, wrote a fantasy and attached John's name to it. If this be the case, then the book has no historical importance for the years A.D. 27-30 or thereabouts. It would be completely untrustworthy as a source of knowledge concerning what Jesus said and did. In this case it would be a book to be despised.

This study of the Gospel is particularly concerned with the substantial contents of the Gospel, the intellectual or doctrinal teaching of the book, the truth that it proclaims, and is not much concerned with matters of higher criticism or Introduction. The questions about the author, date, and so on will not be discussed very thoroughly. However, they cannot be entirely omitted. Some of the evidence will occur incidentally as the contents are considered. For example, on several occasions the text shows that the author had to have been an eye-witness: geographical detail, temporal succession, and minute bits of information are evidences to which historians give weight.

During the last hundred years, and even before 1870, destructive critics have dated the Gospel in the late second century. Bruno Bauer, a New Testament critic of the middle of the nineteenth century, declared that Mark was the first Gospel to be written and that it was written during the reign of Hadrian, 117-138. Consistently he dated John's Gospel later, about A.D. 165. Now, this dating presents a puzzle when one remembers that the Muratorian Canon, a document of A.D. 170, shows that the Gospel was universally accepted; for between Bauer's date and that of the Canon there is not time enough for a fraudulent document to overcome suspicion and be accepted as canonical. If, on the other hand, the Gospel had been published between A.D. 110 and 140, the hundreds of Christians who knew John personally would have denounced it as a forgery. The conclusion is that the Gospel must have been written in the first century.

The late date is no longer so widely held. One of the first scholars to react against this destructive criticism, and one of the best, was my professor of Hebrew in the University of Pennsylvania, James Alan Montgomery, to whose very slender six feet five we students all looked up. The year I began Hebrew with him he published an article, *The Origin of the Gospel According to St. John*, and gave me a copy. After twenty-nine pages of solid argument the pamphlet concludes: "The end of my argument is this: That the Gospel of St. John is the composition of a well-informed Jew, not of the Pharisaic party, whose life experience was gained in Palestine in the first half of the first century, whose mother tongue was Aramaic; and that this conclusion alone explains the excellence of the historical data and the philological phenomena of the book—unless indeed, with Burney, we must argue to a translation of an Aramaic original."

One reason, in addition to its scholarly contents, for mentioning this article is Dr. Albright's comment thirty-one years later.[1] "We have seen that both narratives and logia of

---

[1] Recent Discoveries in Palestine and the Gospel of St. John, *The Background of the New Testament and its Eschatology*, ed. by Davies

John's Gospel certainly or presumably date back to oral tradition in Palestine before A.D. 70. . . . [the oral tradition has been rearranged and edited].[2] But there is absolutely nothing to show that any of Jesus' teachings have been distorted or falsified, or that any new element has been added to them. . . . There is no reason to suppose that the needs of the Church were responsible for any inventions or innovations of theological significance. Whether the Gospel was edited by John the Presbyter of Papias . . . or whether some other reconstruction is more probable, we may rest assured that it contains the memories of the Apostle John—regardless of whether he died in Jerusalem or in Ephesus, though the latter is so well attested by tradition that it remains most plausible."[3]

In a footnote Albright continues, "In this connection I should like to direct attention to an excellent little book by the lamented J. A. Montgomery . . . which deals very intelligently with the limited material then available for the background of the Gospel. I subscribe unreservedly to his conclusions (p. 30)."

Twelve years later Albright wrote,[4] "All the concrete arguments for a late date for the Johannine literature have now been dissipated, and Bultmann's attempts to discern an earlier and later form of the Gospel have proved to be entirely misleading. . . . The date which I personally prefer is the late 70's or early 80's, i.e., not more than thirty or forty years after the composition of the earliest Pauline epistles."

For these reasons and arguments suggested in these quoted paragraphs, one need give no credence to the accusation of Benjamin W. Bacon, in his *The Gospel of the Hellenists*, that the tradition in favor of the Apostle's authorship is "naturally suspect." What is suspect is Bacon's imaginations. He systematically disparages external evidence and accepts as historical his own subjective fancies. For example, he claims that John 1:6-8 was not in the original, but was inserted by

and Daube, Studies in Honour of C. H. Dodd, Cambridge, 1954, pp. 170-171.

[2] Albright has a strange fondness for oral tradition, even when none is needed.

[3] The remark on John's dying in Jerusalem is directed against R. H. Charles' assertion, in his work on *Revelation*, that the Apostle John was martyred before A.D. 70. Charles, of course, is intent on denying the Gospel's authenticity. But even if John had been martyred at that date, he could still have written the Gospel because there is no internal evidence against dating it before the destruction of Jerusalem. This consideration meets Charles' position, for if he rejects the external evidence putting John in Ephesus twenty years later, he leaves for himself only internal evidence for the date.

[4] *New Horizons in Biblical Research*, Oxford 1966, p. 46.

an editor (p. 243). No manuscript evidence supports this invention. Similarly with John 7:37-44 and 10:7-10. Not willing to search for the meaning of the text, as the manuscripts have it, he devises his own meanings and rearranges the order of passages to suit his idea of what an editor would do. Some of his deletions are parenthetical remarks—as if the original author could not have made parenthetical remarks.

The dating, and the significance of the dates, of the extant manuscripts can well be omitted from a study of John's theology. But one point may be included. A tiny scrap of papyrus, called P 52, has three verses of John on one side and two verses on the other. It cannot have been written after A.D. 150, possibly earlier. Because of evidence such as this, even a radical critic like R. H. Fuller has said of John's Gospel, "The date is certainly not later than 100, as the Roberts fragment P 52 shows."[5]

A second subject of discussion has to do with the words we read in our printed gospels, i.e., the words we read in the printed Greek editions. Are these the words of the original manuscript? Or have they been so altered by copyists over the centuries that there is no reason to suppose that John wrote them? This is a very professorial question, even for those who know Greek. Fortunately, the professors with their papyri sheets and vellum codices can answer this question with comparative ease. But the manifold details are not for the general reader.

A third subject of discussion is the question whether the Gospel pictures Jesus as Messiah, divine, the Son of God, and the second Person of the Trinity. The initial question is not whether Jesus is the Messiah. It is not even whether Jesus claimed to be Messiah. These matters are later implications; but the initial question is, Does this Gospel present Jesus as Messiah? Geerhardus Vos in his *Self-Disclosure of Jesus* examined these matters thoroughly. His discussion covers all four Gospels and he analyzes all the nineteenth century theories on these points. One of his conclusions is that these theories exhibit a strong and suspicious bias. The present study pays little attention to these nineteenth century details. The text is quite clear on the main issue. Nevertheless there remain questions of exegesis and inference. Of course, parts of the story are so clear that misunderstanding is almost impossible. Therefore this present book will not be a commentary. There is little use heaping up comments about the obvious; and there are enough commentaries. But many of the puzzling passages can well be examined over again. This sort of discussion will form a large part of what follows. It

---

[5] *A Critical Introduction to the New Testament*, London, 1966; p. 177.

cannot all be original. Nothing written on John today can be original, unless it be something very bad. But what is written here will be about as original as most studies of John, and may prove somewhat helpful. At least the writer hopes so.

Critical problems (author, date, and historicity) and the interpretation of puzzling passages overlap. Is the author a Jew? Does he talk from an Old Testament background? Or does he introduce Greek philosophical speculation into the Christian church? For example, why did he begin with the Prologue, and what does it mean? Did he reject or aim to correct the accounts of Matthew, Mark, and Luke? In this last question matters of historicity and interpretation are intertwined.

Or, further, maybe the question of historicity should not be raised at all. Maybe it does not matter. The gospel can be an impressionistic picture, the result of a mystical, non-verbal revelation. Its aim may not be to convey to us any information, but to produce impressions on us. The accuracy is irrelevant. All that counts is the subjective emotions that are stimulated. Albert Schweitzer proposed a Christianity that lives out of the experiences and energies of an immediate religion that is independent of every historical ground. Emil Brunner wrote, "The witness to the resurrection is not an eye-witness but a faith-witness. It does not inform us of the resurrection, it attests it." Brunner makes even more puzzling statements: "The account of the apostle of his meeting with the risen one is not the basis of the revelational witness, but a phase of it. This phase is the basis of our belief in Christ and therefore of our belief in the resurrection." He continues, "We could believe in the resurrection even if there were no reports of it, so long as we remember that we have the apostolic testimony only because the apostle met the risen Lord, and without that testimony we could not believe" (*Die christliche Lehre von Schöpfung*, pp. 439-441).

This raises the whole question of what revelation is. Did Jesus tell us the truth? Did John write the truth? What is truth? Well, John has something to say about what truth is. Maybe some people will not believe what John says; but it is neither scholarship nor honesty to make him say what he does not say. The first thing to do here is to examine the text. And this will be done.

The scope of these problems is ample and profound. Some very elementary remarks will also be included, even some sermonic material. For that matter, why should not scholarly exegesis be sermonic material? Most humble believers do not have the opportunity to study the destructive critics. But they must meet their influence. It is pervasive. Popular attacks on Christianity are based on the theories of Strauss, Renan (to mention some antiques), Brunner, and

11

Bultmann. The background should be made known. But elementary material is also necessary for background. Over the past twenty years I have quoted a Bible verse as the basis of an exercise in logic. In all these college classes, I think I have found only one student who knew that the statement came from the Bible. I hope that people who attend church, or at least good churches, know a little more. But for the sake of college students, this book will contain some elementary material. Each reader must take what suits him.

Before plunging into anything difficult or profound, one does well to note in a general way what John's purpose was in writing this Gospel. To be sure there is no doubt about the purpose, for John states it clearly: "These things are written that ye may believe that Jesus is the Christ, the Son of God, and that believing ye might have life through his name." Although this statement of purpose is so explicit, still a little preparatory explanation will provide the background for the study of the details to come.

For one thing, could not this statement of purpose be made of Matthew, Mark, and Luke? Was John the only disciple who wanted to convince people that Jesus was the Son of God? Hardly; and yet there is a difference in emphasis and in execution, a difference that makes the purpose especially appropriate for John. There are several differences.

The first difference, and the most obvious, is that Matthew, Mark, and Luke all give a somewhat extended account of the three years of Christ's ministry. They may not have written what nineteenth century historians would call a Life of Jesus, but in their fulness they approximate a biographical account. John, on the other hand, does not give an extended account; although it is he rather than the others who makes it clear that Jesus' ministry covered a three year period. Yet John selects out of these three years only about twenty days. In fact, one third of the Gospel, Chapters 13-19, occurs all in one day. Naturally the day of crucifixion must loom large in any Gospel. Therefore there is a certain amount of overlapping between John and the other three. But as for the other nineteen days, John seems to have deliberately avoided (with one main exception) repeating the events recorded in Matthew, Mark, and Luke. There was, of course, no need to repeat. Therefore Bultmann's argument is valueless, when he says that John either never heard of the Virgin Birth, or, if he had, repudiated it. When John came to write his Gospel, late in the first century, the other Gospels were already well known and widely circulated. A comparison will show that aside from the Passion week, which obviously no Gospel writer could omit, there are only two clear contacts with the other three Gospels, namely, the feeding of the five thousand and the walking on the sea. This difference shows John's

12

independence of the other writers. He did not intend to set them aside, to correct them, nor even to supplement them. Of course, he does supplement them, but that is not his purpose, nor does his method imitate theirs.

The second difference between John's Gospel and the others (which are in technical language called Synoptics because they have the same point of view) is a difference in method or procedure. John relied on personal reminiscences. He was an eye witness and he wrote about what he saw and heard. The other Gospel writers were not eye-witnesses, or at least were not to the same extent. Matthew no doubt observed nearly everything after the time he became a disciple. But Mark could have seen only a little. The Muratorian Canon says that Luke never saw Jesus. John, however, depends on a vivid memory and reports many apparently trivial details. These are signs of an eye-witness. He notes accurately the passage of time (something Matthew is not interested in at all); he gives precise geographical locations; he tells us that the water pots at Cana were made of stone. He tells us what he saw; and, of course, and above all he saw Jesus—but he does not say it just that way. He says (1:14) "We beheld his glory, the glory as of the only begotten of the Father, full of grace and truth." And through the Gospel he tells us what he and the other disciples saw with their eyes, what they heard, and what their hands handled of the Word of Life.

A third difference between John's Gospel and the Synoptics has already been implied. In limiting his personal reminiscences to the events of twenty days, John fills his Gospel with a different content. As was said before, there are only two clear points of contact (not counting the last week). The difference in content lies in this: the Synoptics with their more extensive coverage of Christ's ministry, give a more public view of Christ. They show us Christ before the multitudes. John too in certain places speaks about the crowds; but he chiefly describes lone individuals before Christ. The crowds recede into the background and John centers attention on the impression Jesus made on a few individuals.

There was Nathaniel, who in a few minutes confessed, "Thou art the King of Israel." There was Nicodemus, who had to go home and think a while. There was the woman of Samaria, who accepted him as the Messiah; and the people of the village who said, "Now we believe, not because of thy saying, for we have heard him ourselves and know that this is indeed the Christ, the Savior of the world." Then, to jump ahead, there were the officers who were sent to arrest him: they came back and reported, "Never man spake like this man."

These officers, naturally, are not a lone individual. While

13

the confrontations with lone individuals stand out vividly in John, there are some instances also where groups play an important role. The officers just mentioned, the five thousand who were fed, and the Pharisees are such cases. In this last case Jesus as always made a vivid impression, but it was not a favorable impression. In Chapter 6 Jesus stirs up opposition. The teaching in the temple, given in the next two chapters, resulted in an attempt to kill Jesus. The man born blind, whose eyes were opened, frustrated and infuriated the Pharisees. The raising of Lazarus was intolerable; and the result was that they preferred Barabbas to Jesus.

These three differences between the Synoptics and John, namely, the difference in extent, in method, and in content, all depend on a fourth and basic difference, a difference in purpose.

Matthew's purpose, so it seems, was to convince the Jews that Jesus fulfilled Old Testament prophecies. To do this, he ignored the chronology of Christ's ministry (of course, he began with Jesus' birth and ended with the resurrection; but in between he pays little attention to time) by giving a sample of Jesus' preaching in Chapters 5, 6, and 7, by then continuing with a series of miracles, and later by collecting a number of parables. Mark wrote a short account of Jesus' ministry, presumably for the Romans, chiefly. Luke was particularly interested in chronology. No doubt he (Matthew and Mark as well) hoped that people would come to believe on Christ because of his writing; but Luke had more of an historian's desire to set down the facts "in order," presumably chronological order. Luke's immediate purpose was to assure Theophilus of the certainty of his Christian instruction. Evangelism and the effect of the book on unbelievers is not mentioned.

But John in his Gospel is the evangelist par excellence. Stationed in the city of Ephesus, with its pagan worship of Diana, the scenes of his young manhood come back to the aged John, and before he departs this world he writes his final book, the Gospel, selecting the material so that its readers, including those of all future centuries, might believe that Jesus is the Christ, the Son of God, and that believing they might have life in his name.

## Chapter 2
## THE PROLOGUE

To the ordinary devout Christian who simply wants to study through the Gospel of John, it must seem extremely unfortunate that the first five verses are so extremely difficult. One thus discouraged at the outset may well skip this passage and pass on to easier paragraphs; but let him not forget that he has skipped what John thought the best introduction to his message. There is no compelling reason why a person should not begin with Chapter 3 or 4, or 5 or 6; but he must return, if he wishes to understand the Gospel, for the first five verses are as important as they are difficult.

Since verse 1 is both difficult and important, since indeed the *Logos* is the subject of the present study, the general reader, though he has forgotten his High School Latin and has never had Greek, should patiently spend a few minutes on the mysteries of translation. The most pedestrian way to begin is to list the dictionary meanings of the Greek word *Logos:* "In the beginning was the Logos." What can *Logos* mean? Jerome, whose translation was superior to all previous Latin translations, translated it as *verbum,* and this became *word* in English. But *verbum* is not the cognate form of *Logos. Verbum* is a digammated form of the Greek *eiroo,* and *eiroo* is the root for *rheema,* not *Logos.* Later in this study *rheema* will be considered. But here we try to translate *Logos.* Is *word* a good translation?

Liddell and Scott (edition of 1940), the most thorough of all Greek lexicons, has about five-and-a-half columns, ninety lines to the column, on *Logos.* Some of the meanings listed are: computation, reckoning, account, measure, esteem, proportion, ratio, explanation, pretext, plea, argument, discourse, rule, principle, law, hypothesis, reason, formula, definition, debate, narrative, description, speech, oracle, phrase, wisdom, sentence, and at the very end, word.

Because of this long list of possible choices, because also of the etymological twist of Jerome's translation, and because the usual English translation conveys no meaning to the average mind, *word* is a poor translation in verse 1. "In the beginning" will remind a Bible student of creation in Genesis; but *word* suggests virtually nothing. There is indeed an English word with the same root as *Logos.* Though it would make a somewhat inadequate translation, it would convey some meaning, a relatively accurate meaning; but for a peculiar reason, which this study hopes to dispel, many people dislike it. But to begin in schoolboy fashion, let us try to pick a word from Liddell and Scott's list. Should the inexperienced translator write, In the beginning was the reckoning? Or, In the beginning was the pretext? The hypothesis, the debate? Clearly the list of possible meanings, the list all by itself, is not of much help in arriving at a good translation. One must know how the word *Logos* was used in Greek literature.

In addition to its use in ordinary language, *Logos* in Greek became a technical term of philosophy. Inasmuch as hostile critics have argued that Christianity owes as much or more to pagan Greek philosophy and religion than it owes to the Old Testament, that Paul was actually an initiate of the mystery religions and from them derived the idea of redemption, and that the Gospel was the result of a century of legendary accretions, it is well to compare John's use of the term *Logos* with its use in pagan thought. This latter is part of the larger problem. It contributes to the decision as to whether the doctrine of the Trinity is a pagan construction and whether the words *Hypostases* and *Ousia* in the Nicene Creed come directly from Aristotle and the Neoplatonics. These wider questions, however, must be laid aside now, for the immediate problem has to do with the term *Logos.*

*Logos* became a technical term in philosophy because of the work of Heraclitus, a Greek scholar who lived in Ephesus about 500 B.C. He thought that the universe was made of fire. The evidence is that everything is constantly changing, and fire is the fastest moving of the four elements; therefore all things must be made of fire. But throughout the constant flux, there is a universal law that does not change. Heraclitus called it the *Logos.* This law is indeed the original fire itself. It is a wisdom that directs the course of nature. For which reason Heraclitus says, "It wills and it wills not to be called Zeus."

The Stoics, whose school was organized about 300 B.C., took over Heraclitus' doctrine and developed it. For them too the universe was made of fire, and the cosmos would end in a universal conflagration. At the present time this fire takes on the form of mountains, animals, men. That is to say, a spark of the divine Logos controls or even is each individual thing. These sparks, or *logoi,* seminal logoi, are thought of as seeds, from which grow all that we see. The Stoics may have emphasized, for religious purposes, that every man is a spark

16

of divinity; but the theory requires that animals and mountains be sparks of divinity as well. Clearly Heraclitus and the Stoics were what we usually call pantheists. Certainly the Apostle John did not take over Greek pantheism when he used the word *Logos*. Kittel in his immense *Theological Word-Book* rightly says that "There is a great difference between Hellenistic Logos speculation and the New Testament Logos" (*in loc.* p. 90).

One of the most important differences is that the pagans did not say that their Logos was incarnate in one particular man at a given date in history. True, their Logos was, in a sense, incarnate in every man and animal. It manifests itself throughout the world. But for that very reason it has no unique manifestation, as John describes Jesus Christ. For the Stoics the activity of the Logos is entirely natural, repeated in every event; not something that occurred only once.

Philo, a Jewish philosopher in Alexandria at the time of Christ, made great use of the term *Logos*. He may have been influenced by Stoicism, but he was more influenced by Plato. Plato himself hardly had any Logos doctrine. For him a logos was a verbal expression of thought. Plato did assert the existence of supersensible Ideas in a world above this visible world. The world of Ideas was Plato's highest reality, even superior to the Demiurge (God?), who was the Maker of heaven and earth. Philo, with as much Jewish background as Platonic, represented the world of Ideas as ideas in the mind of God something Plato explicitly denied. This world of Ideas he called the Logos, the Son of God. But his language was extremely figurative, and it is a reading back into him of Christian notions to think that he anticipated John or Athanasius. His language, however, was favorable to Christian (mis-) interpretation.

In addition to these reputable philosophers, the Stoics, Plato, Philo, there were about this time a number of popular religions, called mystery religions. They were mixtures of all sorts of notions. Among these, after the advent of Christianity, particularly in the second century, Gnosticism became a widespread religion. In contrast with the earlier mystery religions, Gnosticism made use of several Christian terms. Since Gnosticism was so widespread in the second century, it must have had its beginnings in the first century. Hostile critics have tried to explain Christianity as a form of Gnosticism, rather than Gnosticism as partly dependent on Christianity. This ties in with the attempt to date the Gospel of John in the late second century. But now that the late date has been discredited, the fanciful reconstructions of the destructive critics are seen to have reversed the historical sequence.

For the explanation of John's Prologue, however, there

remains the problem of why he used the word *Logos*. If this term is to be understood as an element borrowed from Greek philosophy, if John's thought is construed as similar to that of the Gnostics and the Hermetic literature, it is strange that the further and frequent occurrences of the word in John are so totally devoid of such meaning. If, on the other hand, *logos* is simply an ordinary Greek word with all the meanings that Liddell and Scott list, and if John's thought and even the word itself have an Old Testament background, then a very different picture comes into focus.

Not that John was unaware of the philosophic use of the word. There remains one more thing to say about Gnosticism. Gnosticism flourished in the second century. By implication it must have appeared in some form in the first century. Evidence from the New Testament itself (Ephesians, Colossians, and the epistles of John) corroborates this inference. This situation may help to explain why John wrote his Prologue. If we suppose that Gnostic ideas were growing in popularity before A.D. 90, it seems reasonable that a Christian author, not to say an apostle, might warn his readers against false views of the Logos. There were such false views. The so-called Hermetic Literature, with Poimander as its first tractate, describes the Logos as emanating from a Light that is later identified as the Father-Intellect. The Logos is called the Son of God. Poimander's theology is extremely confused and contrasts with John's clarity. For example, some phrases in Poimander seem to teach that the Logos was not "in the beginning"; while others can be interpreted as implying that he was. One sentence says that the Intellect brought forth man co-equal with himself. This is obviously inconsistent with John and the New Testament. Even if one at first sight doubted that Poimander would have made man and God co-equal, and if therefore one wished to minimize the assertion, there can be no doubt that Poimander's salvation is a deification quite different from anything found in the New Testament. It requires egregious stupidity to suggest that the theology of Poimander had any influence on John's or Paul's theology. And although Poimander is usually dated about A.D. 125, there is as little reason to suppose that it derived any of its ideas from the New Testament.

Nevertheless, with such ideas in circulation, there is nothing absurd in supposing that John deliberately wrote his Prologue to warn his Gentile Christians against false forms of the Logos doctrine.[1]

But there is some Old Testament background as well. When the Jewish scholars in Alexandria about 200 B.C.

---

[1] Cf. Clark, G. H., *Selections from Hellenistic Philosophy*, Crofts, 1940, pp. 184-218.

translated the Old Testament into Greek, they had to decide how to speak of the word of God. The Hebrew root is DBR. What Greek word should be used for *word*? From Genesis to Ruth the Jewish translators preferred the Greek word *rheema*. This word and its relation to *Logos* must be discussed later. In the prophets, however, the Alexandrian translators preferred *Logos*, in fact, much preferred *Logos*. Hence even from the standpoint of the Jewish background, John had reason to use this term; but the way he used it in the Prologue can, I believe, best be explained as a denial of pagan religions.

Now, in summary, the ordinary meanings of the Greek term, i.e., the list in the lexicon, can fairly well be combined into the idea of thinking, or the expression of thought. The English cognate is Logic, the science of valid reasoning. As a Greek philosophic term, *Logos* indicates a supreme intelligence controlling the universe. To be sure, this was pantheistically conceived by Heraclitus and the Stoics, but in more orthodox fashion by Philo. And, tautologically, the Old Testament gives the Biblical meaning. Therefore, if one hesitates to translate the first verse as, "In the beginning was the divine Logic," at least one can say, "In the beginning was Wisdom." This translation is accurate enough; it preserves the connotations; and it conveys a satisfactory meaning to the average mind.

There are modern themes also to which the idea of the Logos applies. Two such applications are the German romanticism of the very early nineteenth century and the twentieth century Arianism of Jehovah's Witnesses. John said, with an evident reference to the first verse of Genesis, "In the beginning was the Logos (the Word, the Reason, the Wisdom) . . . and the Word was God." Jehovah's Witnesses refuse to say that the Word was God, and the German romanticists refused to say that God was Word or Reason. First, consider a very interesting passage from Goethe's *Faust*.

> 'Tis writ, "In the beginning was the Word!"
> I pause, perplexed! Who now will help afford?
> I cannot the mere Word so highly prize;[1]
> I must translate it otherwise,
> If by the spirit[2] guided as I read.
> "In the beginning was the Sense!"[3] Take heed,
> The import of this primal sentence weigh,
> Lest thy too hasty pen be led astray.
> Is *force* creative, then, of Sense the dower?[4]
> "In the beginning was the Power."
> Thus should it stand; yet, while the line I trace,
> A something warns me, once more to erase.
> The Spirit aids! From anxious scruples freed,
> I write, "In the beginning was the Deed!"[5]

Certain explanatory footnotes are needed. (1) Faust or Goethe is a romanticist. For him life is deeper than logic. Value consists in having the greatest possible number of experiences—except intellectual experiences. Life is "green" and all theory is "gray." Therefore John is wrong in saying that Reason or Logic is the beginning of things. (2) The spirit, the earth-spirit, anything but the Holy Spirit, guides him to think that Sensation is the source and explanation of all. (3) As the earth-spirit expresses Goethe's pantheism, so sensation is an expression of romanticism. Yet sensation is not accurate enough. Faust, of course, seeks sense pleasures; but he also seeks other varieties of experiences. He wishes to dominate over other people and over all situations. Therefore (4) the source of all had better be identified with power.

*Ist es der Sinn, der alles wirkt und schafft?*
*Es sollte stehen: im Anfang war die Kraft!*

Sense cannot produce and manage everything: it is Power that sometimes works through sense. (5) But Goethe still is not quite satisfied. The best way to translate John and explain the universe is to say, In the beginning was the Deed. This apparently is a reference to the philosophy of Fichte. Chronologically this seems possible because Goethe took a long time to compose *Faust*. Fichte's philosophy was public knowledge before Goethe finally sent *Faust* to the printers. The two men surely agreed on some points. Fichte had difficulty in distinguishing himself from God; his *Ich* and his God were the same thing. This fits Goethe's pantheism. Then too Fichte stressed the freedom of man. Spinoza's intellectual determinism repelled him. It is not science, not intellect that gives access to reality, but faith, a free choice. True, Fichte emphasized morality, and Goethe did anything but. Yet Fichte's emphasis is as much a free, subjective choice as is Goethe's. Thus Goethe seems to be saying that the autonomous choice of man is the beginning of all things. Of course, one must not foolishly suppose that Goethe could not translate a line of Greek. It is not a matter of translation. It is a matter of opposing the Christian view of the universe.

If such is the case with romanticism, the second group of people mentioned above, Jehovah's Witnesses, are back on the level of school-boy translation. The romanticists could not believe that God is Logos. The modern sect cannot believe that the Logos is God.

Jehovah's Witnesses have produced the *New World Translation of the Holy Scriptures*. In it John 1:1 reads, "Originally the Word was, and the Word was with God, and the Word was a god." An appendix supports this translation, first, by a reference to James Moffatt's *New Translation of the New Testament*, where he attacks the Deity of Christ by translating the verse as " . . . and the Word was divine." Secondly the Appendix explains the grammar behind the translation: "The reason . . . is that it is the Greek noun *theos* without the definite article, hence an anarthous *theos.* The God with whom the Word or Logos was originally is designated here by the Greek expression *ho Theos, theos* preceded by the definite article *ho,* hence an articular *theos.* Careful translators recognize that the articular construction points to an identity, a personality, whereas an anarthous construction points to a quality about someone."

The zealous Jehovah's Witness who comes to your front door will repeat all this to you in the best pedagogical fashion approved for professors of Greek. Then if you have a copy of the Greek New Testament beside the door, you can hand it to him and ask for further explanation. A friend of mine did just this. I never quite had the opportunity. When a Witness caught me once with a Greek book in my hand, it was one of Plotinus's *Enneads.* The *Enneads* are very difficult Greek, and it was a dirty trick to ask a Witness to show his knowledge of Greek by translating Plotinus. But it is not reprehensible to offer a Greek Testament to one who presumes to teach you about anarthous predicate nouns in John's Gospel. So my friend put a Greek New Testament in his hands. The man looked at it carefully. Then he turned it up side down and examined it again. Then, *mirabile dictu* (pardon me, that is Latin, not Greek), he turned the Testament on its side and looked at the lines now in vertical columns. Then he asked, What is this? My friend replied, That is a Greek New Testament, about which you have been talking.

Probably my friend did not quote *Goodwin's Greek Grammar,* which says, "A predicate noun seldom has the article." I am fairly sure he did not quote Aristotle 403 b 2, "The definition is the form." Here *form* is anarthous. He might have quoted I John 4:16, "God is love." Or, John 1:49, "Thou art the King of Israel"; where, as in all these cases, the predicate noun is anarthous (cf. John 8:39, John 17:17, Rom. 14:17, Gal. 4:25, and Rev. 1:20).

Since the time of Goodwin, Ernest C. Colwell has done more work on predicate nouns; and he proposes the following rule for the New Testament—"A definite predicate nominative has the article when it follows the verb; it does not have the article when it precedes the verb."

Colwell's studies and their application to Jehovah's Witnesses have been well written up by Robert H. Countess in the *Bulletin of the Evangelical Theological Society,* (now called the *Journal,* etc.) Vol. 10, No. 3, Summer 1967.

The Deity of Christ is, as has been stated, the main message of the Gospel of John. To mistranslate the first verse is to misconstrue the whole book. Yet the first verse of John

21

is not by any means the only passage where the Deity of Christ is taught, either in John or in the New Testament as a whole. Since Jehovah's Witnesses make Christ a created angel, it is well also to show them Hebrews 1:5, "To which of the angels said he at any time, Thou art my Son, this day have I begotten thee?" But as for John the theory of the Logos is not completed in verse 1. The great difference between the pagan theories of the Logos and the Christian Logos is that in the latter the Logos became flesh and dwelt among us. At this point the section on the Logos may end, and what remains can be placed under the exegesis of John 1:1-14.

John wanted to write of the ministry of Jesus Christ. The literary problem was to select a suitable introduction. The relationship between the Son and the Father that John will describe in many places in the Gospel naturally suggests a starting point in eternity. Therefore John's first two words are *en archee*, in the beginning. These are also the first two words of the Old Testament in the LXX translation. This reference to the Old Testament is one of the many reasons for refusing to accept the thesis that John's message is an adaptation from pagan Greek philosophy or religion. It is also an evidence that the subject of which John speaks is God: In the beginning God. Yet Jehovah's Witnesses are right to the extent of indicating that here in John there is a distinction to which Genesis does not allude. They say that the Logos cannot be the same as the God (with the article) with whom the Logos is. They conclude that the Logos therefore cannot be God.

The words *same* and *different*, however, are very flexible words. A cat is the same as a dog in the fact that they both have four feet. A square is the same as a circle in that they are both geometrical figures. When I was a boy there was a shoe polish called "three in one." What precisely was the three and what the one, I do not remember; but there is no contradiction in saying that the same thing is three in one respect and one in another. Later on Jesus will say, I and my Father are one. When therefore John, or any author, makes a puzzling statement, perhaps to attract notice, it is not sound procedure to assume right off that he has contradicted himself. Some authors do indeed contradict themselves. Others think clearly; and if one grasps their thought, one will understand their logical consistency. Hence there just may be some sense in which the Logos can be *with* God and also be God.

Having now asserted the eternal identity of God and the Logos, John in verse 3 makes explicit the reference to creation. Here so soon is the second piece of evidence that the author did not get his ideas from pagan sources. They had no notion of a fiat creation, such as Genesis describes. For that matter, why should anyone search through the pagan religions to find the sources of John's thought? Some of these critics seem to forget completely that the first Christians were all Jews. Why should they not use the Old Testament?

Verse 4 says, "In him was life." The *was*, repeated from verses 1 and 2, is taken by one commentator to refer to the time of creation. In verse 5, however, the present tense occurs in the verb *shines*. Somewhere between verse 3 and verse 5 there must be a shift away from the time of creation to the present, even if it is a general present, rather than the particular time of John. Hence it is not clear that verse 4 must be restricted to a time before the fall of Adam.

With this understanding of the tenses the verse says that the *Logos* was and still is the source of life. This life is hardly physical life: mere physical life was taken care of under the previous reference to creation. Rather under the figure of speech that "this life is the light of men," intellectual life must be meant. If anyone wishes to add moral life, well and good. Moral life is subordinate to intellectual life, for animals, who are below the level of reason, cannot be moral. That the life referred to is rational life is supported by both verse 5 and verse 9, as will become clear, as well as by the previous main thought that Reason, Wisdom, or Logic is God.

In anticipation, some emphasis should be put on the idea that intellectual life is life. Some people do not think so. Romanticism said, Life is green, all theory gray. Schleiermacher and Kierkegaard introduced this notion into the stream of Christian theology. But it is not a Christian notion. John has something important to say about life; but one must not read Kierkegaard and romanticism back into the Gospel.

The life that was in the *Logos*, the creator, was the light of men; and the light shines in the darkness. Verse 5 surely cannot refer to physical darkness. The remainder of the Gospel squarely opposes any such literal view. The light is spiritual and the darkness also is spiritual, rational, or intellectual. This understanding of the verse, along with the present tense *shines*, indicates that at this early stage the Gospel has advanced beyond the time of the creation of heaven and earth.

Again with this understanding, the moral or spiritual darkness did not comprehend, understand, or grasp it. The Greek word is *katelaben*. It means to grasp, to catch on. In colloquial English also the term *catch on* has an intellectual sense as often as or perhaps more often than its purely physical sense of holding something in one's hands.

Weymouth translates the verse, "the darkness has not overpowered it." Although this is grammatically possible, this particular meaning of the Greek verb does not occur in the

23

New Testament; and such meaning conflicts with the parallel expressions in verses 10, 11, and 12.

With a look back to the German romanticists and a look forward to present day mystics and dialectical theologians, this introductory paragraph is inimical to the theme that "life is deeper than logic." There is no hint, as yet at least, that the message of John will be self-contradictory, illogical, irrational. There is no such idea in the Old Testament. One may confidently expect the New Testament to continue the same way. Reason is the source of life; life is not the source of Reason. The evolutionary view of man, which makes rationality an accidental biological development, finds no support in the Bible.

The transition from verse 5 to 6 seems abrupt, but the connection is that John the Baptist came as a witness to the light. John was not himself the light, but a witness to the light—this is clear enough; but verse 9 is a little difficult. A very literal translation is, "It was the true light, which enlightens every man, coming into the world." A new translation, called *A Contemporary Translation*, puts it, "The true light that gives light to every man was coming into the world." This is not a very good translation. Whether it is a good interpretation must be considered.

The point at issue is the identification of the noun which the phrase "coming into the world" modifies. Is it the light that is coming into the world, as the ACT has it, or is it every man who comes into the world, as the KJ says?

The simplest grammatical construction is to connect the phrase with the noun man. As the literal translation given above shows, the participle *coming* is the very next word after the word *man*. To make it refer to a word some distance before complicates the interpretation. Of course, this is possible, but it can be accepted only if there are very good non-grammatical reasons. One reason given is that the Apostle wished to emphasize Christ's coming and incarnation. This, of course, is true, especially if one suspects that John aimed to repudiate the pagan naturalistic theories of the Logos. But with respect to verse 9 the reason is inconclusive because, first, the incarnation is sufficiently emphasized in verse 11, and particularly in verse 14. Verse 14 does not need a weak anticipation in verse 9. Then, second, the light has always been in the world. The imperfect tenses of verse 4, and even of verses 1 and 2, and possibly verse 9, indicate a function that has been carried on since the creation of man. Therefore it seems more likely that verse 9 refers to this function of long standing as it has affected every man that comes into the world.

The sense of the verse, not too easily determined from the verse all by itself, seems to be that Christ enlightens every man ever born by having created him with an intellectual and moral endowment. Paul in Romans 1:32 says, "Who knowing the judgment of God. . . ." The heathen of past ages all know that God punishes immorality. This knowledge is a part of the image of God in which God created Adam. Although this intellectual or spiritual endowment has been defaced and distorted by sin, yet it has not been annihilated: it remains as the basis of human responsibility and renders men inexcusable. Augustine in his *De Magistro* develops other phases of Christ's teaching function.

This light need not mean the light of salvation; in fact it cannot in the verses quoted. Light as a term is comprehensive. It can include actual salvation. But how much light a given passage refers to must be determined by the passage itself and the context.

The verses rush on. The Gospel begins in eternity. Then the creation. Then in verse 5 there is the fall, or at least the results of the fall. Then John the Baptist comes to witness to the Light that the darkness did not grasp; and the author proceeds quickly to the historical Jesus. Christ's coming and his rejection is a case of the darkness not receiving the Light. He came to his own inheritance, to his own possession, Israel, the chosen nation; but the people, his own people did not receive him. And this results in the author's expounding some very important theology.

Verse 12 says that in contrast with the Jews who rejected him, Jesus gave to those who accepted him the right or power to become children of God. These people are identified by the fact that they believe in his name.

Some paragraphs above care was taken to show that the Apostle did not get his message from pagan sources. Greek philosophy and Greek religion did not produce the Gospel. But if it is necessary to distinguish the Christian message from ancient themes, it is also necessary, and more so for people today, to contrast Christianity with much modern religion. For nearly a century the universal Fatherhood of God and the universal brotherhood of man has been proclaimed as the essence of Christianity. In view of these immediate verses in John, it is surprising that such a notion ever should have arisen. Of course, Jesus teaches the Fatherhood of God; but it is not the universal kind of Fatherhood that modern theology has in mind. Modern theology, like the Stoic theory, believes that God is the Father of all men, and that all men are his children. But if words are ever clear, verse 12 asserts that some men are not children of God and that God gives to some others the right to become children of God. They were not God's children before; but now they can become such.

There is a very curious twist in modern theology. Christianity with its doctrine of creation insists on the biological unity of the human race. All men are literal descendents of Adam and Eve. But as Augustine so well explained in the *City of God*, the human race is broken into a spiritual duality. There is the city of this world, and the City of God. Between Stalin and the Apostle John there is no spiritual unity. Yet the liberal evolutionism that characterizes much that passes for Christianity cannot assert the biological unity of the human race. According to the evolutionary theory it is quite possible that human beings evolved from lower species at different times and at different places. Without such a biological unity how can the liberals assert the spiritual unity of the race and preach the universal brotherhood of man? How can they be sure that no higher species will arise with less spiritual unity than men now have?

In opposition to modernism and humanism Christianity asserts that only those who believe in Jesus Christ have the power, the right, or the authority to become children of God. Later on it will be seen that Jesus says that those who do not believe on him are children of the devil. He minces no words: You are of your father the devil, and his works you do; since he is the father of lies, you are naturally liars! But rather than refer to a passage several chapters in advance, it is enough to proceed to the immediately following verse.

Verse 13, a most interesting verse, connects with the preceding "to those who believe on his name," and adds, "who were born, not of bloods, nor of the will of the flesh, nor of the will of a man, but of God."

A few modern commentators have played with a Latin version plus a half a dozen Latin authors who make the verse read, "who was born. . . ." Thus they try to find a reference to the Virgin Birth in the singular verb and the singular relative pronoun. The argument is that the plural, "who were born," interrupts John's line of thought. The emphasis, so they say, is on Christ, not on believers; and to contrast the natural birth of men with their spiritual birth does not serve the main purpose of the paragraph. But, so they continue, a reference to the Virgin Birth in the phrase "not of bloods," a peculiar plural, makes the progress of the thought clear and plain.

One great objection destroys this argument: no Greek manuscript has the singular verb and relative pronoun; and conjecture does not outweigh evidence. The singular occurs only in a Latin version.

As for the progress of thought, it is undeniable in the first place that John is indeed interested in the spiritual birth of believers. Chapter 3 puts this beyond discussion. In the second place, the first chapter, in the preceding verse, has spoken of those who receive Christ, so that believers have

26

already been brought into the picture. Then, third, a reference to the Virgin Birth would put verse 14 out of joint. It is in 1:14 that we have the general statement of the incarnation: the Word became flesh; a particular account of *how* the Word became flesh might have followed the general statement, but could hardly have preceded it.

Geerhardus Vos, in his attempt to find the Virgin Birth in John, does not insist on the singular, though he strangely calls the argument for it "strong." He tries to compromise by suggesting that even the plural reading refers *implicitly* to the Virgin Birth because, if John had in mind *only* the spiritual birth of believers, he simply would have said, "Who were born not of flesh, but of God." The redundancies, "not of bloods, nor flesh, nor a man," indicate a comparison between the believers' new birth and another supernatural birth.

Here Vos, in spite of all his other excellencies, indulges in subjective speculation, and his conclusion could be rendered plausible only by showing that no other interpretation of the so-called redundant phrases is possible. But not only is there another interpretation: it is a much better one.

The primary meaning of the text is that the believer is born of God and is not born of something else. These believers were given the authority, or privilege, or power to become the children of God (cf. 5:27 and 17:2). They did not previously have this power. It was a gift, a gift that God gave to some people and not to all people. This is the Calvinistic doctrine of unconditional election. Now, the so-called redundant phrases make this thought still clearer. If one asks, in view of verse 12, how Christ can be "received," the first part of the answer tells how Christ cannot be received. The first way not to receive or believe on Christ is the way of bloods. The plural doubtless refers to parents, and as such could have formed a contrast with the Virgin Birth, if the Virgin Birth had been there to form a contrast with. As it occurs, however, it directly denies the common Jewish conception that salvation depends on physical descent from Abraham. That this was a common opinion is seen from Matthew 3:9, where John the Baptist upbraids the Jews for thinking that they are safe because "we have Abraham as our father" (cf. also Gal. 3:7). Even today there are some people who rely on a godly heritage of one sort or another.

The second way not to become a child of God is "the will of the flesh." The term *flesh* is regularly used to designate sinful human nature. All men by birth are estranged from God. Hence there is no capability in generic human nature by which a person can become God's child. Then in the third place, this birth is not the result of "the will of a man." That is to say, no individual in the human race stands out so unusually gifted or meritorious or strong of will that he can become a believer in Christ. Some people think that a man is regenerated because he wills to be, and others are not regenerated because they do not will to be. Here it is stated that a man's will has nothing to do with regeneration. John says pointedly that the only way is to be born of God. Human initiative counts for nothing because there is no human initiative. A man believes because he first has been made alive. Just as in natural birth, it is the parents and not the baby who cause the birth, so too in the spiritual realm, it is God and not the man who causes spiritual life, belief, and the status of child. How fortunate! For otherwise the dry bones would not put on flesh, the dead would not rise to newness of life, and the carnal mind at enmity with God could never become his child.

These ideas are so important that the introduction of an obscure reference to the Virgin Birth spoils the sense.

Now comes the culmination of John's Prologue. Verse 14 has two parts. The first part is, "The Word became flesh and dwelt among us." This culminating idea, the great idea that differentiates the Christian Logos doctrine from every pagan philosophy and as well from the semi-Jewish Philonic doctrine, is the incarnation of the Word, the Reason, or the Wisdom of God. The Logos became flesh. So utterly contradictory and even repulsive to all pagan Greek speculation is this that one is astounded to read reputed scholars who characterize John as Hellenistic and dependent on Gnostic, Stoic, or Platonic sources.

For example, consider the views of Edgar J. Goodspeed (*An Introduction to the New Testament,* University of Chicago Press, 1937). Giving the late date of A.D. 110 to the Gospel, Goodspeed asserts that various considerations "combine to show that its author was a Greek, not a Jew" (p. 315). The chief part of this combination is represented in the following quotations. "Greek genius . . . adopted the struggling Christian faith and became its standard bearer for a thousand years. . . . To meet the needs of this Greek public . . . was there no way [to] be introduced to the values of the Christian salvation without being forever routed, we might even say detoured through Judaism? The old books of Christianity were unsuited to this new situation. . . . Matthew . . . how unpromising! . . . The times demanded that Christianity be transplanted to Greek soil and translated into universal terms. The Gospel of John is the response to this demand" (pp. 296-298).

Before continuing with other quotations from Goodspeed, one will note that there is a certain amount of truth in what he says; but there is also a great deal that is erroneous. Of course, it is true that the membership of the church

28

became predominantly Gentile, and that these Gentiles had been raised in a Greek or Hellenistic civilization. But can it be said that in the hundred years after A.D. 70, which marked the end of the early Jewish period, "Greek genius adopted the Christian faith"? Hardly. The Gentile Christians by and large were inferior intellectually even to the decadent Stoic, Aristotelian, and Platonic schools. Later on Origen, not one of the most stalwart defenders of the faith, might through courtesy be called a "Greek genius"; but Athanasius was not; and Augustine could not even read the Greek language. More important is the fact that the most orthodox theologians did not find their themes and concepts in pagan philosophy. Athanasius' *De Decretis*, his defense of the Nicene Creed, seems never to mention Plato or Aristotle, and refers to the Stoics only three times, in a derogatory manner; while there are hundreds of references to the Old and New Testaments. Now, if some Neoplatonic influence is discerned in Augustine, who, remember, received his intellectual capital while he was yet a pagan, a careful reading will disclose that his writings progressively contain less and less of it.

In the next place Goodspeed petulantly asks, "Was there no way . . . [to] be introduced to the values of the Christian salvation without being . . . detoured [!] through Judaism?"

Contrast this with the much more honest appraisal by Karl Barth: "Both in the early days and more recently there have been many proposals and attempts to shake off the so-called Old Testament altogether or to reduce it to the level of a deutero-canonical introduction to the 'real' Bible (i.e., the New Testament). . . . Neither in the New Testament nor in the documents of the second century post-apostolic period do we find the slightest trace of anyone seriously and responsibly trying to replace the Holy Scriptures of Israel by traditions of other nations. . . . Even Marcion never plunged in this direction, although he was near enough to it. We cannot plunge in this direction . . . without substituting another foundation for the foundation on which the Christian church is built . . . as R. Wilhelm has suggested . . . and many recent fools in Germany" (C.D. I, 2, p. 488) and Chicago.

As for the Gospel of John itself, it does not present the Old Testament as a "detour." Consider the reference to Isaiah in John 1:23; and the great verse in 1:29, "Behold the Lamb of God that taketh away the sin of the world." Then there is Jesus' statement, "For if ye believed Moses, ye would believe me; for he wrote of me. But if ye believe not his writings, how shall ye believe my words?" Of a book that so fully mirrors the Jewish, even the priestly, milieu, how can one say that "the Gospel of John is the response to this demand" to avoid the Old Testament detour?

The continued quotation comes from the same page:

29

"Jesus is more than the Messiah of Jewish nationalistic expectation; he is the Logos—the Word of Revelation that came upon the prophets, and also that Reason by which the Stoic philosophy found its way to truth."

Now, it is perfectly correct to say that Jesus was more than the Messiah as conceived by "Jewish nationalistic expectation" at that time. For one thing he was the Messiah as conceived by the Old Testament. It is also true, and the present writer wishes to emphasize it most particularly against its underemphasis in anti-intellectual theologies, that Jesus is the Logos, the Word of Revelation, that not only came upon the prophets but that created the universe. But one must deny that Jesus was the Reason by which the Stoic philosophy found its way to truth. As Athanasius indicated, Stoic philosophy found very little truth. Their materialism and their empiricism is not what the Logos taught them. This is not to deny that Jesus is the Reason that enlightens every man, Hindu as well as Stoic, who comes into the world. The point is that Stoic philosophy, and Platonic philosophy, in their integrity, are not the sources of Johannine theology written to satisfy the stated demand.

On the next page (p. 299) Goodspeed says, "In the Gospel of John the function of Jesus is not so much sacrificial as to bring life and impart it. . . . Jesus' death has little of its old sacrificial meaning."

On the contrary it is clear from the verses last quoted, viz., John 1:29 and 5:46-47, that Jesus' death has all of the old sacrificial meaning. One should also reflect on 4:22, "Salvation is from the Jews," for this pointed answer to the Samaritan woman's question envisages the whole sacrificial system of Leviticus. But Goodspeed plasters over his antagonism to sacrifice by the vague comparison "not so much sacrificial as to bring life." This is the logical fallacy of false disjunction. Jesus brought and implanted life by his death on the cross. There is here no either-or, but a both-and. The sacrifice was essential to the new life.

Goodspeed also holds that John rejected the idea of a final judgment, so graphically portrayed in Matthew. His reason is the statement, "God did not send his Son into the world to pass judgment upon the world," and "the judgment of this world is now in progress" (John 12:31).

As before, Goodspeed's failure to think logically is evident. We could wish that the Logic that enlightens every man had been more effective in this case; but then we do not see the end from the beginning as God does. At any rate, the two verses Goodspeed quotes do not imply that John rejected the idea of a final judgment. At most the second verse implies that the final judgment is not exhaustive of God's judicial procedure: there is also a present judgment. Besides, Good-

30

speed's translation of the Greek is not very accurate. Had he paid attention, he might have recognized that the word *now* does not require the idea of some extended progress, as if this judgment extended throughout history. It is true that there is a divine judgment throughout history. Romans 1:26 reflects on such a judgment. But if one should pay attention to the context in John, one would see that the judgment referred to was the crucifixion of Christ. This assertion, the assertion that the world is judged by Christ's death, does not imply a rejection of a final judgment. The first verse Goodspeed quoted serves him no better. Once again, "God did not send his Son into the world to pass judgment upon the world," does not imply the rejection of a final judgment. It might seem more reasonable to infer that if God did not send his Son to judge, God thereby reserved the final judgment for himself. Hence the idea is not rejected by the text. So much for possible implications. The context, however, gives the reasons and indicates the correct implication: God's immediate purpose in the incarnation was to save the world; there was no need for Jesus to condemn the world, for it was condemned already.

Not only are logic and the immediate context ignored, what is worse, the actual teaching of John on the final judgment is suppressed. First of all there are the verses of 5:28-29, "Do not be amazed at this, for a time is coming when all who are in their graves will hear his voice and come out—those who did good to the resurrection of life, and those who did evil to the resurrection of judgment (or, condemnation)." Then there are the several verses in Chapter 6 that refer to the resurrection at the last day. Besides, Martha, whom Christ had taught, said, "I know he will rise again in the resurrection at the last day." True, in this last passage Jesus says, "I am the resurrection and the life," but Goodspeed's attempt to turn this into a denial of a final judgment is worthless. Can one imagine Jesus or the author John saying, "Martha, you are wrong. Lazarus will never rise again; he has had life in me already; nothing more follows."

As Goodspeed approaches the conclusion of his chapter, he summarizes: John "is in short one of those men who care more for truth than for fact (p. 306); Topography and chronology were among the least of the author's concern" (p. 310).

Now, the distinction between "fact" and "truth" is a tenuous one, and in two other volumes I have discussed the philosophical problems involved.[2] Nothing here, on a colloquial level—and Goodspeed seems to speak colloquially—

---

[2] *The Philosophy of Science and Belief in God;* and, *Historiography: Secular and Religious.*

contradicts the other discussions. It is true then that John cares more for truth than for fact. The "truth" that Jesus is the Lamb sacrificed to God for sin is more important than the "fact" that Jesus one day sat on the edge of a well, thirsty. But in this sense Matthew, whom Goodspeed contrasts with John, also cares more for truth than for fact. The falsity of Goodspeed's paragraph, and the proof that his ambiguous words are not to be taken in their true sense, comes in the next sentence: "Topography and chronology were among the least of the author's concern." Even this may be true literally; but the implication is clear that John paid no attention to topography and chronology and got his facts all mixed up. Had Goodspeed desired to improve his contrast between John and Matthew, he could easily have shown that Matthew did not intend to write a chronological account of Christ's ministry. John clearly did. Indeed, a conservative commentator, Plummer for instance, can well argue from John's meticulous attention to detail to the conclusion that the author must have been an eye-witness of the events. To be sure, the fact that the waterpots were stone and not clay is of less concern than the miracle, but still he noted that they were stone. Et cetera.

Goodspeed then argues that the Gospel is a product of Greek civilization in its attempt to avoid the detour of Judaism because the Jews never carried on conversations. Only Greeks did. There are many conversations in John, and "this trait stamps the Gospel of John as distinctly Greek in feeling and method" (p. 308). For support Goodspeed appeals to Plato and Aristotle. He fails to note that there are no conversations in Aristotle, and that there are conversations in Matthew as well as in John.

The main line of the present volume's discussion had come to the culmination of the Prologue; and this excursus on Goodspeed arose from the liberal inference that John based his views, not on the Old Testament, but on Greek civilization. The greatest refutation of this claim is the culminating verse, "The Word became flesh."

Liberal interpretations of the verse itself and the complex of ideas therein reflected are also surprising. Bultmann[3] writes, " 'The Word became flesh.' . . . The Revealer appears . . . as a definite human being in history: Jesus of Nazareth. His humanity is genuine humanity: 'the Word became flesh.' Hence John has no theory about the preexistent one's miraculous manner of entry into the world, nor about the manner of his union with the man Jesus. He neither knows the legend of the virgin birth nor that of Jesus' birth in

---

[3] *Theology of the New Testament*, Vol. II, pp. 40-42.

Bethlehem—or if he knows them, he will have nothing to do with them."

Before the more important material on these pages from Bultmann is quoted, three remarks can be made on these preliminary lines. The first point is Bultmann's inference introduced by the word "Hence." Surely from the fact that Jesus' humanity was genuine and not docetic, it does not follow that John had no "theory" or notion about the preexistent one's miraculous entry into the world. Bultmann's inference is fallacious. Even the weakening qualification of the last phrase quoted, "or if he knows them . . . , does not remove the illogic of the passage. It is true, of course, that John's Gospel does not give an account of the Virgin Birth: it does not give any account of his birth. But this is not to say that he will have nothing to do with it, as if he repudiated Matthew and Luke. Even Bultmann cannot leave unqualified his suggestion that John, writing perhaps thirty years after Luke, "knows neither the legend of the virgin birth nor that of Jesus' birth in Bethlehem." Of course, he knew them (though not as legend or myth).

The second point is whether Bultmann accepts even the statement, "the Word became flesh." He talks about a "preexistent one's . . . union with the man Jesus." This suggests that either there were two persons, the Word and Jesus, or that an impersonal Word, some divine principle or power, came to indwell the merely human Jesus. In either case Bultmann cannot work into his theory the teaching of John that the Word who created all things and is himself God became flesh.

The third point was somewhat covered under the first. In showing the illogicality of Bultmann's inference, it was also made clear that John cannot be accused of never having heard of Matthew and Luke. Now, to continue the quotation: "Though Jesus says in departing from the earth, 'I have manifested thy name to the men whom thou gavest me out of the world,' still he has imparted no information about God at all, any more than he has brought instruction about the origin of the world or the fate of the self. He does not *communicate anything*, but *calls men to himself.*"

The first chapter of the Gospel contains important information about the creation of the universe, the spiritual plight of man, the nature and mission of Christ, and something of Old Testament prophecy. The occurrence of this information does not contradict the quotation made just above because these verses are the words of John and not of Jesus. Bultmann claims that Jesus offered no information. On this two things should be said. First, a Christian cannot permit himself to be restricted to the ipsissima verba of Jesus, as if the author's words were less true, less authoritative, less important. Red-letter Bibles, if they do not strain the eye-sight, have some small use; but only a small part of Christianity is found in the red sections. In the second place, there can be no objection to asking the question, Did Jesus himself impart any information about God? Did he only call men to himself without instructing them concerning their state and their fate? Did he *communicate* nothing at all?

Well, obviously he communicated several bits of information; and Bultmann himself quotes a part of it. Jesus, in the verse Bultmann cites, informs his disciples that God has given him a certain group of men chosen from out of the world's population. In fact, Chapter 17 contains considerable information about God. It tells us that God gave authority to Jesus to give eternal life to those people God had chosen. Eternal life is defined as knowledge of God. God sent Christ into the world. All that belongs to God belongs to Christ. And a second time, God sent Christ into the world. God is in Christ and Christ is in God. Again, God gave Christ a certain people. God loved Christ before the creation of the world. These several items of information about God, to which no doubt a few implications could be added, are by themselves enough to contradict Bultmann's rash assertion that "Jesus . . . has imparted no information about God at all."

If one should summarize all the information about God that Jesus imparts in the Gospel as a whole, the account would be lengthy; yet it is of use to list some other items of information that Jesus communicated about God, the origin of the world, and the fate of the self—nothing of which occurs in the Gospel, according to Bultmann.

Though the first reference will be one of the poorer references, for the exact words are not given, Jesus convinced Andrew (John 1:41) and Nathaniel (1:49) that he was the promised Messiah, the Son of God, and the King of Israel. Let Bultmann refer to this as calling men to "himself"; it is also theological information.

The conversation with Nicodemus, more explicitly than the previous verses, records a quantity of theological information. Jesus informs Nicodemus that God requires a man to be born again before he can enter God's kingdom. After continuing with this idea for ten verses, Jesus informs Nicodemus that he must be lifted up as Moses lifted up the brass serpent; that those who do not believe on the Messiah shall perish; and that he is the Savior. Jesus also informs Nicodemus of the evil of loving sin rather than righteousness. Granted, this is not explained in full; granted also that Nicodemus did not understand the good news; granted even that it says nothing explicit about the origin of the world; but it is nevertheless news, information, and theology about God and the fate of the self.

Chapter 4 recounts the information Jesus gave to the woman at the well. No doubt he revealed *himself;* but he did so by giving information. This information included the fact that he was greater than Jacob; that he supplies "water" better than Jacob's; it also includes his supernatural knowledge of the woman's life, with the implication that he is a prophet; he also very plainly informs her that salvation comes through the Jewish nation and that up to the present God requires his people to worship him in Jerusalem and not on Mount Gerizim; there follows the information that soon worship no longer will be restricted to Jerusalem. Then Jesus gives the woman the information that God is spirit and explicitly tells her that he is the Messiah. All this presupposes the truth of the Old Testament and therefore asserts divine providence through the course of history. How then can Bultmann write that Jesus imparted no information at all about God, about himself, and the fate of the self? He certainly cannot maintain his position on the basis of the text.

Chapter 5 gives information about the relationship of Jesus to the Father. Important as it is, need it be detailed here? It is strong trinitarian theology. The chapter also contains information about the Old Testament, much more explicitly than Chapter 4. Next, Chapter 6, among other things, gives information about the resurrection of believers: surely this comes under the category of the "fate of the self." And as for solid, profound, and even disturbing theology, there is verse 44. It was disturbing information to the Jews because many of them who had followed Jesus to this point could not accept the theology here given and now deserted him because of it (6:65-66).

Without going tediously further into the later chapters, one can now conclude that the documentation against Bultmann is overwhelming. There is, however, a slightly amusing point. Though Bultmann distinguishes between what Jesus said and what John says, apparently preferring Jesus' own words, yet his favorite verse, "the Word became flesh," is one piece of information that Jesus did not communicate: these are the words of John. Is Bultmann then willing to accept all of John's statements as true, as "Gospel truth"; and if he is not, why should he so much prefer this one?

No further criticism is necessary; but two more paragraphs, twenty some pages later, show the ingrained wrongheadedness and perversity of Bultmann's treatment of John. "Jesus' words never convey anything specific or concrete that he has seen with the Father. Not once does he communicate matters or events to which he had been a witness by either eye or ear. . . . So it is clear that the mythological statements have lost their mythological meaning. Jesus is not presented in literal seriousness as a preexistent divine being who came in human form [i.e., the Word did not become flesh; worse, John himself did not mean that the Word became flesh].... Practically all the words of Jesus in John are *assertions about himself* and no definite complex of ideas can be stated as their content and claimed to be the 'teaching' of Jesus.... His words are assertions about himself. But this does not mean christological instruction or teaching about the metaphysical quality of his person."

That all this is wrong-headed is clear three times over. First, Bultmann's assertion that Jesus not even once relates what he has seen with the Father contradicts several passages. John 5:19 and 7:16, if they do not concretely mention the things Jesus saw with the Father, none the less state that everything that Jesus taught was seen by him with the Father. John 8:25-28 presumably refers to what Jesus has just said, but can imply all the rest of his teaching too. All this teaching is what Jesus saw with the Father. John 12:49 indicates that what Jesus said in the preceding verses, including the prediction of a final judgment, are parts of God's commandment to him. Similarly John 14:24 refers to the preceding context.

Second, Bultmann's statement that practically (?) all of Jesus' words are assertions about himself is partly false and totally irrelevant. It is partly false (depending on how one understands the *practicality*) because Jesus asserted the Mosaic authorship of the Pentateuch, the need of a new birth, and something about the spiritual position of Abraham. It is also irrelevant because there is no reason why Christ should not have spoken about himself. Did he not have to explain who he was?

This leads to the third point. Christ spoke about himself, but says Bultmann, this does not mean christological instruction or teaching about his Person. But why does it not mean this? Jesus said, "I and my Father are one." Note again that Bultmann restricts his remarks to the reported sayings of Jesus. No attention is paid to the narrative or the interpretation of the author who reported them, except at the end of the paragraph where Bultmann concludes, "No wonder then that the evangelist can confer upon him for his preexistent period the mythological title Word (Logos)!" Indeed, with the exception of the one term, mythological, it is no wonder.

"The Word became flesh" is the culminating verse of the Prologue. If Bultmann had succeeded in eviscerating this verse of all its meaning, then Goodspeed would have an easier time in interpreting John as a device to avoid the "detour" through the Old Testament. He would still be defeated, however, by the powerful verses at the end of Chapter 5.

Since therefore the views of these critics cannot be maintained, there remains only the short task of completing the verse and concluding this account of the Prologue.

"The Word became flesh and dwelt among us, and we gazed at his glory, glory as of the only from the Father, full of grace and truth." That Jesus is the only one from the Father sets him and his ministry on a level that the prophets could not attain. The word *only* does not literally mean "only begotten." It means the only one of its kind. This little bit of Greek vocabulary, however, does not weaken the doctrine that Jesus is the only begotten Son. The word *beget* is found in Hebrews 1:5. Therefore the fundamentalist theologian who argued against the eternal generation of the Son on the ground that the word in John did not mean generation was wrong because he forgot Hebrews.

Nor does the phrase "the only from God" injure the doctrine of the Deity of Christ. If we should continue through the first chapter of John to verse 18, we should find, not that Jesus was the only Son, but that Jesus is the only God. It might seem to make better sense to read verse 18 as "the only begotten Son who is in the bosom of the Father"; but the better text is, "the only God who is in the bosom of the Father." Whatever other difficulties this reading produces, at least it is a most emphatic statement of the Deity of Jesus.

If the Prologue ends at verse 14, this verse is beyond its scope; but it enforces the culminating idea of the Prologue that the glory of the Logos is full of grace and truth.

## Chapter 3
## LOGOS AND RHEEMATA

The obvious importance of *Logos* in Chapter 1 demands an examination of its other instances in the remainder of the Gospel. At the same time there is another term to be compared with it. *Rheema* (singular, though it does not occur in the singular in John) and *rheemata* (plural) mean word and words, ordinarily spoken words. One therefore asks, Are these two terms, *logos* and *rheema*, identical in meaning, contrasted in meaning, or in any way related?

To begin with the etymology previously mentioned, *rheema* has the same root as the Latin *verbum* and the English *word: eiroo*, to say, speak, or tell. It occurs sixty times in the New Testament. *Logos* has the root *legoo:* to say, speak, or tell. It occurs over twelve hundred times. Though the two roots are almost identical in meaning, some modern theologians wish to contrast *rheemata* and *logos*. Investigation of this matter best begins with a list of the instances of each word in John. The *logos* list comes first.

One category of the instances of the term *logos* in John, a noticeable proportion of the total, defines it by giving examples. These make it indubitable that *logos* means a sentence, a proposition, a doctrine, an object of intellectual apprehension. They make it indubitable by quoting the proposition to which they refer.

The first such instance is John 2:22. After cleansing the temple at the beginning of his ministry, and being confronted by the Jewish authorities, Jesus says, "Destroy this temple, and in three days I shall raise it up." Naturally the Jews were nonplused. But "when he was raised from the dead, the disciples remembered it, that he had said this, and they believed the scripture and the *word* that Jesus had said." The word was, of course, the sentence, "Destroy this temple, and in three days I shall raise it up." This sentence is the "it" that the disciples remembered; it is the "this" that Jesus had said. Accordingly the *logos* is this sentence.

The next such case is John 4:37. "For in this the saying (*logos*) is true, that one sows and another reaps." The adage or saying is the *logos*. It is stated to be true; and the only thing that can be true is a proposition or declarative sentence. Two verses below there is the next *logos*. "Many of the Samaritans from that city believed on him through the word of the woman who said that he told me everything I have ever done." The *logos* is precisely the sentence, "He told me everything I have ever done." Another two verses down "Many more believed because of his preaching." Here in John 4:41 *preaching* or *argument* is a good translation for *logos*. The actual words are not quoted, but the verse refers to two days of discussion and preaching that Jesus engaged in with the Samaritans. Still in the same chapter, but no longer concerning the Samaritans, John 4:50 tells us that the nobleman, who came to Jesus and requested him to heal his son, "believed the word Jesus said to him." The *logos* was, "Your son lives."

In the sixth chapter Jesus preaches about the bread from heaven. He also refers to eating his flesh. Then in verse 60, "Many of his disciples, when they had heard, said, This doctrine is difficult; who can accept it?" *Logos*, here, although in the singular, must not be translated by "a word." Nor even by "a sentence." The reference is to the whole sermon. And if anyone dislikes the translation, "This doctrine is difficult," he may translate it, "This sermon is difficult." But the meaning is the same, for it was the intellectual content that caused the displeasure of the audience.

John 7:36, 40 are similar. In the first of these the *logos* is the assertion, "You will search for me, but you shall not find me." In the second, the plural occurs: "Some of the crowd, when they had heard these words, said, "This man is indeed the prophet."

Restricting this section to instances where a definite sentence or sentences define the *logos*, we come next to John 10:19. Here Jesus had just said that he lays down his life voluntarily; no one can take it from him. "Then the Jews, because of these words (*logoi*), were again divided." The words referred to are roughly all of the first eighteen verses.

In several cases the *logos* is a verse in the Old Testament. John 12:38 quotes Isaiah 53:1. John 15:25 quotes a part of Psalm 35:19 and Psalm 69:4. John 18:9 refers back to John 6:39 and 17:12. In this case the prophecy fulfilled was one that Jesus himself had made. The same essentially is true of John 18:32, where the words referred to are in John 3:14, 8:28, and 12:32-34. They are not actually quoted, but the *logos* is these assertions. The *word* is singular, and hence can be translated *thought, idea, doctrine,* or best, the *words* in the plural. Finally, there is a prophecy, a misunderstood prophecy, that spread among the disciples. Jesus had said, "If I want him to remain alive until I return, what is that to you?" This was the *logos*, the *rumor*, the *idea*, the *thought*. A further instance where *logos* refers to a definite sentence is John 15:20, "Remember the proverb (*logos*) I told you: the servant is not greater than his lord."

Two other instances where the *logos* is identified by an explicitly quoted sentence, though in these cases it is Pilate and the Pharisees who are involved, rather than Jesus, are John 19:8 and 13. In the first of these verses the *logos* that frightened Pilate was "He made himself the son of God." The second of these verses refers to several sentences. The King James version is incorrect in using the singular. *Logos* here occurs in the plural: "When Pilate heard these words. . . ." The words were the declaration by Jesus and the shoutings of the Jews.

Here then is a long list of cases where the meaning of the term *logos* is determined by quoting it. It is always an intelligible proposition.

At this point, and before continuing with the list of instances of *logos*, the reader might want to know what the connection is between the sentences or propositions just given and the Logos of verse 1 who created the universe and enlightens every man who comes into the world. How did the argument get from Christ to sentences? The connection is this: the *Logos* of verse 1 is the Wisdom of God. To him his worshippers erected the architectural triumph Hagia Sophia, the church in Constantinople dedicated to the Holy Wisdom of God. To purloin Heraclitus' phrase, this is the Wisdom that steers the universe. But this steering, the plan on which the universe is constructed, the providential governing of all creatures and all their actions, is based on wise counsel. God does not work haphazardly. He acts rationally. Some of this wisdom is expressed in the propositions of the previous list. They are the mind of Christ: they are the very mind of Christ. In them we grasp the holy Wisdom of God. Accordingly there is no great gap between the propositions alluded to and Christ himself. The Platonic Ideas, as interpreted by Philo, and by him called Logos, are the mind of God. Some of these Ideas are given to us in the words of John, or in the words of Christ recorded by John. This is how Christ communicates himself to us. Is it completely ridiculous to suggest that this is why John uses the term *logos* for these two, superficially different purposes? But now to continue the list of instances.

Another category can be constructed of those instances where no definite sentence is quoted, but where the reference is clearly to previously spoken sentences. John 5:24 reports that Jesus said, "He who hears my word and believes him who sent me has eternal life." The phrase "He who hears my word," can equally be translated, "He who hears my doctrine"; and it can be interpreted as, "He who accepts my doctrine or theology." Verse 38 of the same chapter says, "You do not have his word remaining in you because you do not believe the one he sent." This verse also refers generally to the doctrine or theology that Jesus had been preaching. John 8:31 and 37 are entirely similar. So is John 8:43, with the additional parallel between *logos* and *lalia*. This latter word means speech or talk. The translation can be, "Why do you not understand my talk? Because you cannot hear [accept or understand] my word." Verses 51 and 52 also use *logos* to refer generally to Jesus' preaching: "If anyone keeps my doctrine, he shall not see death ever." Three verses below Jesus contrasts himself with the Pharisees on the ground that he, Jesus, keeps God's *logos*.

Besides these verses in which the term *logos* refers generally to the preaching of Jesus, John 10:35 uses *logos* to designate the prophecies of the Old Testament. The prophets were men to whom the *logos* of God came, and this *logos* as written in the Scripture cannot be broken. This is the first verse so far quoted that definitely links the *logos* to the *written* words of the Old Testament. The idea that the *logos* is something that can be written down on papyrus, parchment, or vellum is important, even if only because it is so distasteful to the dialectical theologians.

The paragraph before this last one compared *logos* with words, not as written, nor with words merely as such, but with spoken words. John 12:48 identifies the *logos* with *rheemata* or words as such. The passage reads, "He who ignores me [or, sets me aside] and does not accept my words (*rheemata*), has a judge: the *logos* that I have spoken, that *logos* will judge him in the last day." Note that the *logos* is something spoken and naturally therefore consists of words.

If the listing of these verses seems tedious, it is at least overwhelming and leaves no defense for those who deprecate words and doctrine. John 14:23-24 says, "If anyone love me, he will keep my *logos*. . . .He who does not love me, does not keep my *logous* (plural); and the *logos* which you hear is not mine, but the Father's who sent me." The combination of singular and plural, of hearing and therefore of saying, enforces the point of the argument.

Since some fundamentalists also have accepted the anti-intellectualism of the liberals, we must patiently plod through the list. John 15:3 is, "You are already clean because of the theology I have spoken to you." John 17:6 and 14 hardly need to be quoted. Verse 17 says that God's word is truth. And in verse 20 of the same chapter the *logos* referred to is the future preaching of the disciples.

To make this a complete list of all the occurrences of the term *logos* in the Gospel of John, we have only to add

41

John 1:1 and 14. In the beginning was the *Logos,* the logic, the doctrine, the mind, the wisdom of God. The wisdom of God is God. This *Logos* became flesh and we saw the glory of his grace and truth.

Contemporary theology frequently distinguishes between the *Logos* and the *rheemata:* the Word and the words. The Word is in some sense divine. If it is contained in or somehow mediated by the Bible, the Bible is "authoritative," though not infallible. Just how false statements can be "authoritative," the liberals do not explain. Reception of the Word for them is a sort of mystic experience without intellectual content. The words, on the other hand, are human, fallible, and mythological. The supernatural truth of God is so different from human truth that they do not coincide at a single point and not even omnipotence has the power to express it in human language; therefore the words, the concepts, are mere pointers to an unknowable object.

A conservative theologian naturally wants to examine this view and compare it with the words of Scripture. A "Biblical" view could hardly be absent from the Bible.

After the meaning given in the lexicon is stated, the first step will be to list the occurrences of *rheema* in the Gospel of John.

Souter's Greek lexicon translates *rheema* as "*a spoken word, an utterance,* the concrete expression of *logos:* hence, perhaps Hebraistically, a subject of speech, a *matter,* a *thing,* a *fact,* ... in a solemn sense, of a divine *word* ... the Christian *teaching,* the *gospel.* ..." Liddell and Scott do not add anything of great importance, except that in grammar *rheema* designates a verb (verbum) rather than a noun.

Jesus is never called the Rheema, as he is called the Logos. *Rheemata* in a very literal sense are the sounds that come out of one's mouth when one speaks. These are not thoughts; they are sounds in the air; they are the symbols of thoughts. When people belittle "mere words" they confuse the thought with the symbol. In the science of Logic there is a distinction made between sentences and propositions. A proposition is the thought symbolized; the sentence is the symbol. *Es regnet, il pleut,* and *it is raining* are three sentences, but they are one proposition. Any one of the three is a satisfactory symbol of the thought. In linguistics attention is paid to the symbols as such. Medieval philosophy had a theory of second intentions: to say that a cat is an animal is to use the word cat in its first intention; to say that a cat is a noun is to use the word in its second intention. But people other than philosophers and semanticists hardly think about these distinctions. Most of the time they keep in mind the thing symbolized, even though they may mention the symbol. But in an anti-theological epileptical seizure they will sometimes inveigh against mere words, forgetting the truths they stand for. In the present monograph we are not particularly interested in semantics; we are greatly interested in the truths conveyed by the symbols.

*Rheema* first occurs in John 3:34, "The man who accepts the testimony confirms the fact that God is true, for he whom God sent speaks the words of God, for God does not give the Spirit by measure." One notices here that the emphasis is on truth. God is truthful. Therefore the words of God are true, and the Son, who speaks the words, does so because God has given him the Spirit without limit. Here *rheemata* cannot be put on any level lower than the divine *logoi*. The words are spoken under the limitless authority of the Holy Spirit.

The next reference, John 5:47, is one of the most important on the authority of words, both written and spoken. After healing the lame man at the pool of Bethesda, directing him to pick up his rug and walk, and at the climax of the ensuing confrontation with the Pharisees, Jesus (in a stern and awesome voice) exclaims, "Do not think that I will accuse you before the Father. Your accuser is Moses in whom you have put your hope. For if you believed Moses, you would believe me, for he wrote of me. But if you do not believe his writings, how can you believe my words!"

Here Moses appears as an accuser, naturally a legitimate accuser with a legitimate accusation — so much so that Christ himself need not accuse the unbelieving Pharisees. They had refused to believe what Moses had written. Of course, Moses had written words on parchment. These words receive the full approbation of Christ. Thus Christ attributes to Moses' written words the full divine authority of truth. Because the Pharisees do not believe Moses' written words, they cannot believe Christ's spoken words. These words, these *rheemata*, are (in part), "the Son makes those alive whom he wants to . . . the Father has given all judgment to the Son in order that all people should honor the Son as they honor the Father. . . . Indeed I tell you that whoever hears my *logos* and believes him who sent me has eternal life." In these earlier verses the message of Christ is a *logos;* at the end of the chapter this same message is called *rheemata. Logos* and *rheema* designate the same thing.

Although the present study is confined to John's Gospel, Luke too uses *rheema* and *logos;* and in his Gospel as well can be seen the identity of the two terms. *Logos* occurs some thirty times in Luke, four times in Chapter 1. *Rheema* also occurs in Luke 1:37, "No word of God shall be without power." The word immediately subsumed under this universal statement is the prophecy of the virgin birth. As a statement of intellectual content it differs in no wise from the

four *logoi* of Luke 1:2, 4, 20, and 29. In fact, the *logos* of
verse 29 is identical with the *rheema* of verse 37. That this
proposition and all the other informative statements God
makes are not without power means that they are all true.
Nor can they be dismissed on the pretext that God's thoughts
are not our thoughts and that therefore the omnipotent God
has no ability to express information intelligible to man. The
proposition, "Thou shalt have a son" means precisely the
same thing for both God and man. No doubt God knows
other propositions he did not reveal to Mary; but this one
*logos* and *rheema* God intended Mary to understand.

To return now to John, the next occurrences of *rheema*
are found in 6:63 and 68. After giving his discourse on the
bread of life, which if a man eat he will live forever, and
when he perceived that his disciples whispered in discontent,
Jesus said, "The Spirit is the one who gives life . . . the words
that I have spoken to you are spirit and life." Here the words
Jesus speaks are identified as the spirit, or the Spirit, who
gives life. Few people who center their thought on "mere
words" are inclined to identify the words with the Spirit. But
John says that the words are spirit and life.

Since a list becomes tedious as it grows longer, and since
the idea of life is most important, it is well at this point to
emphasize that the words are eternal life. The emphasis will
take the form of a contrast with an epileptic case of anti-
intellectualism. An editorial in *Christian Heritage* (June
1971) states (and I shall quote the paragraph in its entirety to
avoid the suspicion that I have somehow garbled it by omis-
sions), "It is a very strange paradox indeed: unbelievers
cannot leave God alone, believers can and do. Unbelievers
talk against God with zealous fanaticism, whereas believers
hesitate to talk for him precisely because they do not want to
appear to be fanatical. If ever the two confront one another
both tend to recreate God in their own image, that is, they
both underestimate the character of God. One attributes to
him the cruelty and vindictiveness which they feel toward his
disciples, the other reduces their Lord to loveless propositions and barren doctrinal definitions with which they would
brow-beat their faith-less opponents."

The exaggeration of the first part of this paragraph does
not concern us. It describes neither all believers nor all
unbelievers. But it makes clear that the subject of the latter
part of the paragraph is believers and unbelievers. Therefore
the last half of the last sentence, and this is the matter of
concern, means that believers reduce the Lord to loveless
propositions and barren doctrines with which they brow-beat
unbelievers. Since this is said to be true of all believers, and
since the author does not brow-beat people, it would seem to
follow that he is not a believer. But, maybe, he brow-beats

believers, and so qualifies. The brow-beating comes in the words *loveless* and *barren*. The author wants us to believe that Christian doctrine is barren. It has no life, no spirit.

The Apostle John, however, and the words of Christ that he records contradict the sentiment of the editorial. Christ said, "The words that I have spoken to you (the propositions) are spirit and life." To have eternal life is to have these words; and such a life is not barren. The believer is justified by faith, by what he believes. This belief is not barren because justification inevitably and without exception produces sanctification.

In the verses that follow John 6:63 Jesus goes on to tell his disgruntled disciples that no one can believe his words or come to him unless the Father causes him to. This Calvinistic determinism offended the people and many of them deserted Jesus for that reason. But Simon Peter, answering for the twelve, said, "To whom shall we go? Words of eternal life you have! We have believed and we know that you are the Holy One of God." If Christ's discourse is *rheemata*, could *logoi* be any greater?

*Rheema* again occurs in John 8:20; aside from identifying the term with Jesus' claim to be the light of the world, the verse adds nothing further to the argument. More important is John 8:47. The tremendous discourse approaches its climax with the condemnation of the Jews as sons of the devil. He is their father — neither Abraham nor God. Because Jesus tells them the truth, these liars do not believe him. "He who belongs to God hears God's words: that is why you do not hear — because you do not belong to God." Here is the condemnation of our contemporary dialectical theologians. They disparage the words. They do not believe that Christ was virgin born; many of them, e.g., Barth and Bultmann, do not believe in a resurrection at the end of history; they empty the words of their intellectual content and leave them bare symbols to be filled in with foreign meaning. They do not hear the *rheemata* of Christ because they do not belong to God.

The next reference, John 10:21, "These are not the words of a demoniac," does not advance the argument. But John 12:47-48 combines *logos* and *rheema* in one passage. It must therefore be considered. "Jesus cried out and said . . . if anyone hear my *rheemata* and refuse to observe them, I do not judge him. . . . He who ignores and does not receive my *rheemata* has a judge: the *logos* that I have spoken will judge him on the final day." In the section on *Logos* this passage has already been listed as showing the identity of *logos* and *rheemata* — explicitly the fact that *logos* can be a spoken as well as a written word or thought. It is further noteworthy that the *logos* judges the unbeliever on the last day, "the *logos* I have spoken." But the Judge on the last day is Christ himself because "the Father judges no one, but has given all judgment to the Son . . . he has given him authority to judge because he is the Son of Man" (the Messiah). It cannot be an inadvertence on John's part that he here identifies the spoken words with Christ himself. John was not a contemporary semanticist, nor a medieval philosopher distinguishing between "first and second intentions." As a Jew he ignored the symbol as such — a symbol that differs from language to language. John was interested in the thought, the meaning, the truth. And as you and I are what we think, so the Divine Mind is the Truth.

Again, the next reference, John 15:7, "If you remain in me and my words remain in you . . . " adds nothing further to the argument. The final instance of *rheemata* in the Gospel is John 17:8, "I have given them the words thou has given me." These *rheemata* therefore are not just human words infected, as they may be, with sin and error; these *rheemata* are given by the Father to the Son. These same divine words, the Son gives to his disciples. They do not change in the two givings. They are transmitted *in toto* and without alteration from the Father to the Son to the disciple. Therefore the text of the Gospel diametrically contradicts the dialectical theology and all else that minimizes the grasp of intellectual, intelligible truth (there is no other kind) in favor of pictorial mythology and meaningless mysticism.

Chapter 4

TRUTH

An earlier section, the exegesis of John 1:1-14, ended with the idea that the *Logos* was full of grace and truth. There are now two reasons why John's concept of truth should be studied. First, John emphasizes truth. This can be seen, in a preliminary way, in the fact that the term *truth* occurs twenty-four times in the Gospel; the adjective occurs thirteen times; and a less ordinary form of the same root occurs eight times; plus ten or eleven less important cases of the adverb. Numbers alone prove little. The verb *become* occurs at least forty-nine times, but nothing of theological value can be derived from a word-study of *ginomai*. The idea of truth, contrariwise, is of great philosophical and theological moment — as soon will be seen.

Aside from the sufficient fact that John emphasizes the notion of truth, there is a second reason for this study. Contemporary theologians these days often defend a type of "truth" quite different from the ordinary truth that past generations have acknowledged. Heretofore truth consisted of propositions. A truth was a sentence. An example would be, David was King of Israel. A falsehood was also a sentence, such as, David led the children of Israel out of Egypt. Now the twentieth century has invented a new kind of truth, and Emil Brunner, a convenient representative of this type of theology, wrote a book with the title, *Wahrheit als Begegnung — Truth as Encounter*. If I meet a person on the street, that is truth. Truth is not the sentences this person may say to me; it is simply the event of meeting him. The reason for this queer application of the word *truth* to something to which it was never before applied is that Brunner and the dialectical theologians wish to establish a theory of revelation devoid of information, that is, really devoid of truth. Revelation is an event: we meet God. He does not say anything to us; but the meeting itself is revelation and truth. God gives us no information; or if he should give us information, it could be false information because "God can, when he wants to, speak his word to a man even through false

47

teaching" (*op. cit.*, German, p. 88, English p. 117). Revelation itself has no intellectual content; there is nothing to be believed. From this it follows (does it not?) that we do not *know* even that it is God whom we meet. God and the medium of conceptuality, Brunner says, are mutually exclusive.

How untrue Brunner's theory is can be shown by listing and examining the occurrences of the word *truth* in the Gospel of John; and this will reinforce the truth of what has been said and what further will be said about the *Logos*.

The word *truth* (*aleetheia*), as indicated above, occurs twenty-four times in the Gospel. Not every instance is perfectly convincing for the purpose, but the entire list will be given to show that no instance contradicts the conclusion. For example, the first case is not so clear as some others. John 1:14 says, "The Word became flesh . . . and we beheld his glory . . . full of grace and truth." To say that Jesus was full of truth could mean that he was sincere. Even so, sincerity is a state of mind in which the speaker believes that what he is saying is true. But to be full of truth could also mean that Jesus had a great deal of information about God. When we speak of an enthusiastic teacher as being full of his subject, we mean that he knows a lot about the subject, and we use the expression because he is constantly communicating this information. There is no reason to deny that Jesus had a great amount of information to give. As a matter of fact Jesus later said, "I still have many things to tell you, but you cannot hold them now." Surely Jesus did not mean: I must encounter you many more times, but not today.

The second instance is John 1:17, "The Law was given by Moses, but grace and truth came into being by Jesus Christ." The dialectical theologians would doubtless writhe if the next verse were translated: "No one has ever seen God; the only begotten God, who is in the bosom of the Father, this very one has exegeted him." Nevertheless it is a good translation — however much the intellectual work of exegesis or interpretation fails to fit the dialectical notion of Jesus' mission. Verse 18 is surely in some way an explanation of verse 17. The truth that came into being by Jesus Christ is, at least partly, his explanation, interpretation, or exegesis of the unseen Father.

Next, John 3:21 is a verse that is sometimes used to argue that truth is not always intellectual, that there is another kind of truth, and that it is moral obedience. The verse says, "He who does the truth comes to the light in order that his works may be seen to have been done through [more literally, in or by] God." This phrase, "doing the truth," obviously signifies moral obedience. The context contrasts this man with those who do evil deeds and who try to

48

hide them in darkness. The obedient man comes to the light so that all may see that his conduct is godly. This use of the word *truth*, however, gives no support to the dialectical notion of truth as encounter; nor is it so far removed from mind, knowledge, and intellect as the opponents of knowledge and intellect could wish.

Admittedly a moral command is not a proposition and cannot be either true or false. But the context not only refers to light and darkness as revealing or hiding men's deeds from observation; it also takes us back to the Light of Chapter 1 that lighteth every man who comes into the world. This Light no doubt involves moral principles; but since it is the Word or Wisdom of God, rational and theological material is also included. One cannot separate moral principles from logical principles on the ground that the latter are intellectual or rational and the former are not. Moral principles, to be followed, must be known. While then a command as such cannot be true, it is a proposition and a truth that God commands men (for example) not to steal. Therefore there are no anti-intellectual overtones in speaking about *doing* the truth.

The next reference, containing both the noun and an adjective, may seem even more remote from the truth of a proposition. If all the verses were like these, someone might doubt that John's concept of truth had much to do with the cognitive meaning here maintained. But, for one thing, the later references are abundant and clear; and for another thing, John 4:23 requires the intellectual meaning as its background. Jesus was talking with the Samaritan woman. She wanted to know whether people should worship God on Mt. Gerizim or in Jerusalem. Jesus plainly tells her that the Samaritans were wrong: up to the present Jerusalem has been the place that God had appointed for worship. Then Jesus adds, "But a time is coming, and has now arrived, when the true worshippers will worship the Father in spirit and in truth." The same thought and the same word are repeated in the following verse.

Since clearly Jesus is announcing something that goes beyond the Old Testament, and since the Old Testament condemns hypocrisy, these words are not a simple call to sincerity. They indicate a new administration of divine grace in which Jerusalem as a locality is of no importance. This is a truth. To worship God therefore now necessitates a recognition of this truth or proposition. No doubt it goes still further than a mere rejection of Jerusalem; nonetheless such is contained in the meaning. What is further must be the whole New Testament revelation. Since Jesus here announces a new form of worship, his intent, though the particulars remain unexpressed, must envisage the new worship in its

49

entirety. The conclusion is that Jesus explicitly presented the woman with at least two propositions: the sacrifices at Jerusalem have come to an end, and I am the Messiah; and implicitly he had in mind his Atonement and all the rest.

This verse also contains the adjective *true* (*aleethinos*); and rather than repeat the verse under the list of adjectives it is better to finish it here and indeed add several other verses where this adjective occurs. Earlier there was John 1:9 in which the phrase is, the true light. Here, of course, it is the true worshippers. In John 6:32 we have, the true bread. John 15:1, the true vine. John 17:3, the only true God. This adjectival use is a derivative from the basic meaning of the noun. The phrase, it or he was the true light, simply means that the proposition, the Logos is the light, is a true statement. Therefore we must not see in this adjectival use some unusual type of truth by which to disparage the ordinary variety. St. Augustine pleasantly explains this literary form. Phrases such as *the true bread*, *the true light*, and so on, picture the object as saying to the beholder, I am bread, I am light; and this claim is true.

The next instance of the word *truth* is flanked by another adjective *true* (*aleethees*). John 5:31-33 reads, "If I testify concerning myself, my testimony is not true. There is another who testifies about me, and I know that the testimony that he testifies about me is true. You sent off to John, and he has testified to the truth." If the previous references needed a little bit of explanation to show that they referred to propositional truth and not to some other kind, the meaning here and in most of the following references lies on the surface. The situation described here resembles a law court. The witness of one man is not accepted as true; but if two witnesses concur, their witness is acceptable. Jesus has several witnesses, mentioned in various places in John. There is his own witness, the witness of John the Baptist, the witness of Jesus' works, the Father himself, the Scriptures, and in the Scriptures especially Moses. In this section the other witness is not John the Baptist, but the Father, as the following verses show. But the Baptist is referred to in the verses quoted.

The presence of witnesses and the picture of the law court show the meaning of true and truth. A witness makes a statement. It is either true or false. Such testimony in a colloquial manner may be called personal truth. It may be based on a face to face encounter between two men; and it may state something about the character of the person to whom the testimony refers. But it is still a proposition. There is no personal truth that is not propositional. Statements such as, Judas was a thief and, Jesus was the Messiah, are as personal as anyone can rightly demand; but beyond these statements of intellectual or cognitive content, there is no meaning to the word truth.

In Chapter 8 the idea of true witness in a court of law recurs; and although the word *truth* does not occur in verses 12 to 30, this is the best place to take account of these instances of the adjective. The phrases are: thy witness is not true, my witness is true, my judgment is true, the witness of two men is true, and one other of the sort Augustine discussed — he that sent me is true. These verses (13, 14, 16, 17, and 26) with the exception of the last have the same meaning as those in Chapter 5. Nothing further needs to be said, for the thing that is true is the statement made on the witness stand.

The noun *truth* occurs several times in the following section. It will be best to exegete verses 31 to 47.

After discussing the truth of Jesus' witness and his relation to the Father, we read in verse 31, "Accordingly Jesus said to the Jews who believed him, If you remain in my doctrine (*logos*), you are really [truly] my disciples; and you will know the truth, and the truth will liberate you." Although the preceding section ends with the information that many of the Jews believed on him, and although this section begins by referring to the Jews who believed, the present verses indicate either that there were Jews in the crowd who did not believe or that some of them believed only a few detached propositions. Whichever group it was that replied to Jesus, they paid no attention to the truths believed, but stumbled at the idea of becoming free. "They answered him, we are the descendants of Abraham and have never been servants of anyone. How can you say, you shall become free? Jesus replied to them, Most assuredly I tell you that everyone who commits sin is the servant of sin. Now, the servant does not remain permanently in the home: the son remains permanently. If therefore the son liberates you, you will really be free. I know that you are descendants of Abraham; but you seek to kill me because my theology (*logos*) makes no progress in you. I speak what I have seen with my Father; and you do what you have heard with your father."

Note that *truth* and *word* or *doctrine* refer to the information that Jesus had presented in verses 12-30, and possibly to other sermons that he had preached still earlier. It is truth and knowledge that liberate; Jesus does not ask them to have some emotional experience; he requires that they believe.

The conversation continues. "They answered and said to him, Our father is Abraham." Jesus had just said that they did what their father told them to do. As in the earlier verses the Jews can only think of Abraham as their father. But

51

"Jesus says to them, If you are sons of Abraham, you were doing the works of Abraham."

This over-literal translation obscures the sense. One is tempted to use a variant reading, not very well attested, and translate, "If you are sons of Abraham, do the works of Abraham." The best sense appears in a better, but not the best, attested reading: "If you are [or, were] the sons of Abraham, you would be doing the works of Abraham."

"But now you seek to kill me, a man who has told you the truth which I have heard from God. Abraham did not do this."

This is the only place where Jesus refers to himself as a man. The reason is doubtless that they want to kill him, and will eventually do so. Hence it is proper to refer to his human nature, since the divine nature cannot be killed. What is important for the present purpose is that Jesus is a man who has told the truth. It was the truth that angered them; and this truth is the message that Jesus had been preaching. The message, at least the immediate message of the chapter, was a matter of propositions such as: I know where I came from, but you do not know where you came from; and, You judge according to the flesh; You shall die in your sin; You are from below, I am from above. These are simple, ordinary sentences. They are expressions of intellectual content; and that is why Jesus said, I am a man who has told you the truth. Truth consists of propositions.

One of the implied truths is that Abraham is not the father of these Jews. They were not doing the works of Abraham. Instead, they were doing the works of their father. These assertions were not so easy for those Jews to understand, but nonetheless they are intellectual expressions. Since the Jews perceive the inference and understand that Jesus is denying that Abraham is their father, could it be that Jesus is accusing Sarah of adultery? Hardly, for Jesus, a few verses back, had admitted, "I know that you are descendants of Abraham." Then it dawns on these Jews that Jesus is talking about spiritual descent, "so they say to him, We were not born of fornication; we have one father, God. Jesus replied to them, If God were your father, you would love me, for I came from God and here I am; nor have I come on my own initiative, but he sent me. Why do you not understand my language? Because you cannot hear my argument (*logos*)."

Note again that Jesus appeals to understanding a rational argument. It is not an emotional experience or dialectical encounter that he has in mind, but a simple grasping of logical content. Although this is a study of the Gospel of John, it may not be objectionable to quote II Corinthians 4:3-4 because there too is a mention of the inability of people to understand intellectual propositions. Paul writes,

"But if our gospel is hidden, it is hidden in them who are perishing, in whom the god of this world has blinded the thoughts of the unbelievers in order that [*eis* with the infinitive is generally purposive; it can indicate result and be translated *so that*] the light of the gospel might not dawn (on them)." Aside from the interesting fact that ancient Greek used the same idiom as modern English and made *dawn* a picture of the beginning of intellectual apprehension, one must note that the hidden thing is the good news, information, cognitive sentences; and that the work of Satan is not to give these people bad emotions but to prevent them from thinking the right thoughts. The antithesis is entirely intellectual.

Jesus now tells the Jews plainly who their father is. As in II Corinthians it is the devil who blinded the thoughts of unbelievers, so here "You are of your father, the devil, and you want to fulfil the desires of your father; he was a murderer from the beginning," so naturally you want to kill me; "and the platform on which he stands is not truth [or, a little more literally, he has not taken his stand in the truth] because truth is not in him. When he lies, he speaks out of his own resources, because he is a liar and the father of lies. [Since you are his children] you do not believe me for the simple reason that I speak the truth. Who among you convicts me of sin [the sin of lying]? If I speak the truth, why do you not believe me? He who is [the descendant] of God hears the words (*rheemata*) of God. That is why you do not hear: you are not [the children] of God."

In these last few verses the emphasis falls on the antithesis of truth, namely, lies. A falsehood is the contradictory of a truth. If it is true that Alexander the Great died young, it is false that he lived to an old age. If Abraham did not pursue the five kings and recover Lot's goods, it is false to say that he did. If it was a sin to kill Christ, then Caiaphas made a false statement when he said it was better for the Pharisees that Christ should be killed. There is no such antithesis between intellectual truth and morality as some superficial minds imagine. A lie, the denial of a truth, is immoral. It is a sin to think incorrectly. When a person thinks that it is profitable to steal, or when some of the ancients thought they could ward off illness by sacrificing to an idol, their false opinion was sin. There can be no such thing as morality unless there are true moral principles. Morality depends on truth.

Note also in this section that truth is expressed, not only in arguments (*logoi*) but in words (*rheemata*). There is no such antithesis between truth and words as some modern theologians imagine. Jesus said, the child of God hears God's words. Now, very literally, it is the case that words are

53

symbols. The word c-a-t does not look like a thing that meows, nor can it scratch. And *Katze*, though cognate, is not the same symbol. In this sense the word is not "the real thing." But in colloquial speech we usually make no distinction between the word and the concept. The reason is that we are not discussing linguistics; we are merely thinking about a cat. For this reason, Brunner is perhaps half right when he says, "All words have only an instrumental value." But he is all wrong when he adds, "Neither the spoken words nor their conceptual content are the Word itself, but only its frame" (*Divine Human Encounter*, p. 110). According to the Apostle John and according to Jesus, the Word of God, the *Logos*, and the words, the propositions, the cognitive content, are identical; and this conceptual content is "the real thing."

The next references to truth are John 14:6 and 17. Here Jesus tells Thomas, "I am the way, the truth, and the life." Then after several verses in which knowledge is emphasized Jesus promises to send the Spirit of truth, whom the world cannot grasp because it does not know him.

The first of these verses can easily be understood to mean that Jesus is (to use ancient terminology) the World of Ideas, the Mind of God. This accords with the Prologue and there is no reason why it should not. However, while the verse must include this meaning, the context suggests a more immediate application to the difficulties of Thomas. The puzzled disciple does not know where Jesus is going and therefore cannot know the way. Under the circumstances it is not strange that Thomas and Philip were puzzled. It may seem strange that Jesus did not answer them in terms that they could understand. His answer goes far beyond the range of their thought. Nevertheless it includes their problem. I am the way, he says, the way of life; in fact, I am the life; and the reason I am the life is that I am the truth, the World of Ideas, the plan of the universe, and therefore also the norm by which a disciple should conduct himself. The way to know the Father is to know me. And this knowledge is life. Then Jesus promises them another Advocate, the Spirit of truth, whom the world neither contemplates nor knows. Here the idea of knowledge determines the meaning of the word *truth*. It is the object of knowledge. To know the Spirit is to know the truth. Trinitarianism ascribes to each of the Persons all the attributes any of them has. The functions of the three Persons are somewhat differentiated, in that certain functions are more usually ascribed to one Person rather than to the other two, but in truth all three do everything together (excluding the human functions that are the God-man's alóne). Therefore one can say that the Spirit is the Truth and that the Son is the Truth. And surely the Father is not ignorant. Here the relation of truth to the Spirit is probably the fact that teaching is one of the functions regularly assigned to the Spirit. Verse 26 specifies the action of the Spirit in causing the apostles to remember correctly what Jesus had said and done in order that they might write it down without error.

John 16:7 says, "I tell you the truth." The truth that Jesus here tells his disciples is that he is going away. A few verses before, he told them that they would suffer persecution. Several times he emphasizes the fact that he is telling them something. What he tells them is so indisputably information, plain ordinary intellectual content, that to suppose truth to be some mystic encounter is wilful blindness. In verse 12 Jesus says that he has more to tell them: more information, what else? But since the disciples cannot carry it away at the moment, the Spirit of truth, when he comes, will direct them in all the truth. This truth, which the Spirit takes from Christ, the Spirit will announce or report to the disciples. Note that announcing or reporting has to do with propositions. If it be said that one announces people or reports people, a quick glance at the morning's newspaper will show that the announcement consists of propositions.

John 17:17 says, "Sanctify them by the truth; thy word, doctrine, argument, theory is truth." Just a page or two back the *logos*-word and the *rheema*-word were seen to be identical. Thus the truth here that sanctifies is the message of the Scripture. Sanctification is basically an intellectual process. No doubt it eventuates in external conduct; but before one can act rightly, one must think rightly; and so we are sanctified by truth. The idea is repeated in verse 19: "I sanctify myself for them, in order that they may sanctify themselves by truth."

It is hard to see how anyone can be sanctified by encounter. Improvement in conduct, in holy living, in moral action, requires instruction and information. If children have not been brought up in the nurture and admonition of the Lord, if they have not been given normative principles of Scriptural content, an emotional evangelistic appeal or experience can have no Christian meaning. As someone has well said: Christianity is taught, not caught. The Christian message, the truth, comes to a man through his mind or intellect. To believe it, it must be understood. An encounter without propositional content is an hallucination. Or, better, it is not even an hallucination, for an hallucination has content, though false. "That the soul be without knowledge [or, desire without knowledge] is not good" (Prov. 19:2).

Emphasis on knowledge, understanding, and truth is found explicitly in many chapters of the Bible; but the Gospel of John with twenty-four instances of the word *truth*

55

is the book in which the greatest emphasis is found. The remaining three instances now conclude this section.

John 18:37 contains two of these three and the next verse has the final instance. Pilate asks Jesus, Art thou a king? Pilate is asking for information; and Jesus' answer is affirmative. The form of speech is somewhat unfamiliar to English speaking people. It can be translated, "You speak (well) because I am (indeed) a king." The remainder of the verse leaves no doubt that Jesus claims to be a king. Even the form of speech is not totally foreign to English, if we use slang. Then the translation is: "You said it! I am a king." Then Jesus continues, "I was born for this purpose, and for this purpose I have come into the world. The purpose is to witness to the truth." What truth? No doubt many other propositions also, but at least to this piece of information, that I am a king. Then, next, "Everyone who depends on the truth hears my voice."

At this Pilate asks, and it is the last instance in the Gospel, "What is truth?" This question is a little hard to interpret with certainty. Had Pilate been a philosopher, he might have asked, What is the nature of truth — What is the correct theory of epistemology? This would have required the definite article before the noun *truth*, and the article is not in the text. Did Pilate mean, What is the truth in this case before me? Yet, though he may not have believed that Jesus was a king, he was convinced of the truth of Jesus' innocence with reference to the accusations. It seems best to me to suppose that Pilate, though he was not a philosopher, asked about the abstract nature of truth. Jesus had said, not only that he was a king, but that he had come into the world to bear witness to the truth. Here the definite article appears. Pilate seems to have spoken with this in mind, even if he did not use the article. After all, professional philosophers are not the only persons who sometimes think about the nature of truth.

Along with the twenty-four instances of *truth*, seven cases of the adjective (*aleethees*) were discussed. The remaining six are John 3:33, 4:18, 7:18, 10:41, 19:35, and 21:24. They all reinforce what has already been said. Five instances of the other adjective (*aleethinos*) have been mentioned. Three others are John 4:37, 7:28, and 19:35. The adverb occurs ten times. They add nothing further. Truth therefore is propositional, and these propositions we are called upon to believe.

The concept of truth, of eternal immutable truth, is of first importance to Christianity, for without it the gospel would not be true. It could not even be pragmatically useful; for if it were, then it would have to be true that it is useful. Nor could morality exist without truth because, if it is not true that God imposes obligations and punishes disobedience, it would not be true that man is obliged to do anything, nor could any motive for virtue and sanctification exist.

The twentieth century in large measure has rejected truth and has accepted relativism. Joseph Fletcher exhibits the immoral consequences of relativism in his situation ethics. He insists that one ought — and in saying *ought* he contradicts himself, for he cannot justify any *ought* — to disobey every one of the Ten Commandments. It is John Dewey, however, who goes to the root of the matter and provides situation ethics with its philosophical foundation. Dewey insists not only that the "truths" of science and history change, but that the very forms of logic change. Aristotelian logic used to be true. In the past one could validly argue: All Americans are human beings, therefore some human beings are Americans.[1] But now, Dewey asserts, this is no longer valid. If some other elements of Aristotelian logic still remain true, obversion perhaps, they too will sooner or later change. What has been valid will become invalid, and what has been invalid will, at least eventually, become valid. If Dewey does not say in so many words that "All Americans are human beings implies that no Americans are human beings" will become valid, at least he repeatedly denies all limits to change in logic. Since there are no eternal truths in Dewey's philosophy, the absurd inference cannot forever be invalid.[2]

Dewey is a twentieth century example of the reaction against Hegel that set in with Karl Marx and Soren Kierkegaard. The German philosopher Hegel, early in the nineteenth century, exploded Kant's assertion of an unknowable Thing-in-Itself. But in correcting Kant he gave the unfortunate impression that he thought he had discovered just about all the truth there is. His enemies took advantage of this (not altogether justifiable) impression. But in rejecting many propositions that Hegel claimed to have established, a twentieth century movement, including instrumentalists, the dialectical theologians, and the existentialists, rejects the possibility of any fixed, immutable, eternal truth. Not only is this the case with liberals and left-wingers, but some people who consider themselves evangelicals also have tendencies to disparage truth. These men have adopted relativism, not by studying the history of philosophy, for they have not done much studying; but rather, being ignorant of the source, they

---

[1] Or any example with universal premises and a particular conclusion.

[2] Cf. my monograph, *Dewey*, pp. 61-69. Presbyterian and Reformed Publ. Co., 1960; and *Thales to Dewey*, Chapter 11. Houghton Mifflin, 1957.

unwittingly accept ideas that have become popular and fail to perceive how the new views are inimical to Christian truth. So as to avoid generalities, to be concrete, and to rebut in advance the charge of knocking down a straw man, the specific case of A. W. Tozer will be examined. Although Dr. Tozer, in the sermon to be quoted, disparages Fundamentalism, most people who knew him and his denomination, the Christian and Missionary Alliance, would probably classify him as a fundamentalist. Surely he considered himself a conservative evangelical. Furthermore, the sermon from *Tozer Pulpit*, Vol. 3, was reprinted by *The Presbyterian Journal*, February 11, 1970 — a journal that claims to defend orthodox Presbyterianism from the onslaughts of the dialectical theologians. When thus the ostensible defenders of the faith accept the position of the enemy, unwittingly of course, one can measure the strength of the contemporary rebellion against the truth. What is worse, Dr. Tozer appeals to the Gospel of John. The following criticism aims to show that Dr. Tozer and *The Presbyterian Journal* completely misunderstand the Gospel and make it say precisely what it denies.

First of all, Dr. Tozer distinguishes between two kinds of truth, though as in Kierkegaard the second kind is not precisely distinguished. The first kind of truth is the kind the unbelieving Jews had. It is "intellectual merely. . . . I gather this not only from verse 17 [John 7:17, If a man chooses to do God's will, he will find out whether my teaching comes from God or whether I speak on my own] but from the whole Gospel of John. To these people truth was an intellectual thing, just as we know two times two is four." Apparently Dr. Tozer thinks that if doctrine and teaching come from God, instead of from the rabbis, it cannot be intellectual.[3]

---

[3] When the feast was half over, Jesus went into the temple and taught. The Jews were astonished because Jesus had never "learned" in a rabbinical school. If now Jesus had said that he needed no schooling, but spoke on his own authority, the Jews would have called him an imposter. To get their attention Jesus claims to have had a teacher: someone sent him and his doctrine is that taught by the "someone." Note that the word here is *didachee*, a rather technical term emphasizing a "school of thought," a professional view, a claim to authority. If *didachee* is not intellectual, one would have difficulty in saying what is. The "someone" who taught and sent Jesus is, of course, God; and Jesus then tells his enemies how they may learn whether his *didachee*, his theological teaching, comes from God or not. Thus we come to the seventeenth verse from which Dr. Tozer claims to deduce the theory of two kinds of truth. The verse is, "If anyone resolutely wills to obey his commandments, he will know concerning the *didachee*, whether it comes from God or whether I speak on my own." What does this verse

58

For Dr. Tozer's intellectual truth is somehow inferior. "Two times two is four: that is truth, but it is an intellectual truth only. . . .They [the Jews] believed that if you had the words of truth, if you could repeat the code of truth, you had the Truth. That if you lived by the word of truth, you lived in the Truth." There is some confusion here. The Pharisees and all the unbelieving Jews had many sins to account for, but respect for the truth was not one of them. One of the Pharisees' sins was hypocrisy: they did not believe what they said they believed. This makes it hard to know exactly what they believed. But it is not likely that many of them believed that "if you had the words of truth, if you could repeat the code of truth," you had the Truth in any saving sense. They insisted on circumcision; and a Gentile who merely repeated aloud the Mosaic code was not thereby saved. Dr. Tozer is more accurate when he adds, "If you lived by the word of truth, you lived in the Truth." This they believed (let us say); but this is no sin. Romans 2:6-7, 10, 13 definitely assert the principle that Dr. Tozer opposes. Jesus himself, in the Gospel of John, insists on obedience to the truth. The fault of the Jews was not their honoring of the truth as such; if they believed that the truth saves, they were right. Their sin was that what they honored and believed was not the truth. They did not believe Moses and the prophets. It was for this that Jesus condemned them. He did not condemn their alleged rationalism, intellectualism, or respect for the truth. The difference between the Jews and Jesus lay in the propositions to be believed.

Dr. Tozer seems little interested in what a person believes. He is little interested because he has a low opinion of intellectual truth. He wishes to substitute a different kind of "truth." Exactly what it is, he does not make clear; but whatever it is, it is incompatible with evangelical theology and contradictory of John's Gospel. Read the quotation

---

mean? Does it mean, as Pascal said: Go through the motions, say the rosary, attend mass, *s'abêtir*—stupefy yourself, and you will come to believe? Surely this cannot be the meaning. The text does not say, "he who does God's will, will know." Rather, the text speaks of one who is willing to do God's will after he learns what it is. This is not what Pascal had in mind. Pascal's stupefaction consists in going through the motions before knowing that they are God's commands. It seems, rather, that Jesus is directly addressing his Jewish audience in their own situation. They were not willing to obey the Mosaic law. This Old Testament background is explicit in verse 19. Jesus charges them with plotting to kill him. If they had been willing to put away their murderous plot and obey the Ten Commandments, they would have recognized that Jesus' teaching came from God. Or, in other words, taken from John 8:37-41, if these Jews had the faith of Abraham, they would have believed what Jesus said.

carefully. "The battle line, the warfare today, is not necessarily between the fundamentalist and the liberal. There is a difference between them, of course. The fundamentalist says God made the heaven and the earth. The liberal says, Well, that's a poetic way of stating it; actually it came up by evolution. The fundamentalist says Jesus Christ was the very Son of God. The liberal says, Well, he certainly was a wonderful man and he is the Master, but I don't quite know about his deity. So there is a division, but I don't think the warfare is over these matters any more. The battle has shifted to another more important field. The warfare and dividing line today is between evangelical rationalists and evangelical mystics."

Note how Dr. Tozer disparages the difference between believing that God is creator, that Jesus is the Son of God, and presumably other fundamental doctrines and believing that God did not create the world, that Jesus is no more than human, and that a good part of the Bible is untrue. He admits that there is a difference between the liberal and the fundamentalist, but he seems little interested in that difference. This warfare is over — says Dr. Tozer. But for a true Christian, if he has average common sense, this warfare is not over. A true Christian cannot treat the Deity of Christ so lightly, nor the doctrine of creation, either. There may be a sense in which the battle line of the twenties has shifted in the seventies; but it is not such a new field as that between "evangelical rationalists and evangelical mystics." In one sense, a very fundamental sense, the battle line has not shifted at all. The old battle line that centered on Harry Emerson Fosdick's denial of the Virgin Birth and his warning against worshipping Jesus was itself a question of the truth of the Bible. Some people may have seen only that the Deity of Christ and the Atonement were involved. But scholars like J. Gresham Machen saw clearly that the whole Bible and all of Christianity was involved. This is still the battle field. What may be new, since the middle of the nineteenth century, is a view that Truth is not true, and that the Bible instead of being honestly false, as Wellhausen asserted, is dishonestly "true" like Aesop's fables. For the new Truth is simply the old falsehood.

The attempt to belittle intellectualism and the old truth by reducing belief to a mere memorization of words is a misrepresentation that occurs in several places in the sermon. The two are not the same. One can memorize a passage in Spinoza or Karl Marx, without believing it, in fact for the purpose of arguing against them. But Dr. Tozer says, the Jews thought that "if you want to know the truth, go to the rabbi and learn the Word. If you get the Word [by memory, not by belief] you have got the truth. There is today an evangelical

60

rationalism which is the same as that of the Jews" which tells us "If you learn the text, you have got the truth." Now it may be that fundamentalists, not being very well educated and often misunderstanding what the Bible teaches, say some peculiar things; but do any of them mean that memorization apart from belief gives salvation? The trouble here is that Dr. Tozer holds belief in low esteem and therefore tries to belittle it by talking about "getting" the words.

Naturally, once or twice Dr. Tozer uses the word *belief*, for it is belief that he is belittling by reducing it to repetition and memorization. Hence he says, "Your evangelical rationalist . . . says what the Pharisees, the worst enemies Jesus had while on earth, said: Well, truth is truth and if you believe the truth you've got it." What Dr. Tozer fails to notice is that the so-called evangelical rationalist believes that Jesus is the Son of God who gave his life a ransom for many, and the Pharisee believed that Jesus was an imposter and blasphemer. Dr. Tozer fails correctly to evaluate belief because he believes that belief, no matter in what, has little value.

Therefore Dr. Tozer claims that the new and more important battle line is between evangelical rationalists and evangelical mystics. Does Dr. Tozer know what the term *evangelical* means? The Protestant Reformation, i.e., the evangelical movement, has, in Aristotelian language, a formal principle and a material principle. The material principle is the doctrine of justification by faith. The formal principle is *sola Scriptura*, the Bible alone.[4] But a mystic is precisely one who rejects the principle of the Bible alone. He has a source of revelation outside the Bible. Hence there cannot be an evangelical mystic.

Dr. Tozer's unevangelical views and un-Johannine religion are unmistakable in the following quotation.

> There is something behind the text that you've got to get through to. . . . Is the body of Christian truth enough? Or does truth have a soul as well as a body? The evangelical rationalist says that all talk about the soul of truth is poetic nonsense. The body of truth is all you need; if you believe the body of truth you are on your way to heaven and you can't backslide and everything will be all right and you will get a crown in the last day. . . . Just as Colossians argues against Manichaeism and Galatians argues against Jewish legalism, so the book of John is a long, inspired, passionately outpoured book trying to save us from evangelical rationalism, the

---

[4] Cf. The Presidential Address to the Evangelical Theological Society, Dec. 29, 1965, in the Bulletin of the E.T.S., Vol. 9, No. 1, Winter 1966.

doctrine that says the text is enough. Textualism is as deadly as liberalism.

If now the reader will kindly note the points quoted and compare with the criticisms below, he will see the significance of the debate. First of all one must ask whether a man who insists on the truth of God's word, and in fact understands the Bible as well as or even better than most evangelicals is a greater enemy than, as Dr. Tozer says he is, or even as great an enemy as, a man who denies that God created the world and denies the Deity of Christ — the two items by which the quoted author distinguishes between fundamentalists and liberals.

In the second place, does a distinction between the body and the soul of truth have a meaning or is it poetic nonsense? A century or two ago some Puritans wrote books on theology and used the title, *The Body of Divinity*. This title is a figure of speech, yet it has an intelligible meaning. It means the several theological doctrines that the author thinks most important. But when a contrast is made between the truths themselves and something different from them called their soul, intelligible meaning is surely replaced by poetic nonsense. The best evidence of its poetic nonsense is that its meaning cannot be stated in literal language. The meaning of the title *Body of Divinity* can be so stated: it is the several important truths themselves. But neither the author quoted nor others explain what this "soul" is. The author contents himself with disparaging the truth, or the body of truth, without giving any indication of what this other thing is.

Then, third, it is amazing that the author describes the Gospel of John as a passionate attack on "evangelical rationalism." John's Gospel contains at least twenty-four instances of the word *truth*, none of which disparages the truth; it also contains thirteen instances of the adjective *true*, and eight instances of another adjective of substantially the same meaning; in addition to which there are about ten instances of the adverb, some of which, however, contribute little to the present subject. John also lays stress on the *Word* and the *words*, beginning in his very first verse and working up to a tremendous condemnation of the Jews, in Chapter 5, for their refusal to believe the words of Moses.

This passage and others similar show the inaccuracy of classifying "evangelical rationalists" with the Pharisees. The author had said, "Your evangelical rationalist . . . says what the Pharisees, the worst enemies Jesus had while on earth, said: 'Well, truth is truth and if you believe the truth you've got it.' " This attempt to picture the "evangelical rationalist" as the worst enemies Jesus has had since he was on earth fails because the Pharisees did not believe the truth. If they had

62

believed the writings of Moses, they would have believed the words of Christ.

The sermon's appeal to the Gospel of John is so incredible that it is worth while to examine again at least one paragraph of that Gospel. Consider John 8:48 ff.

The Jews had just accused Jesus of being a devil-possessed Samaritan. In rejecting their accusation Jesus says, "If anyone keep my word, he shall never never see death ever." It is to be admitted and indeed insisted upon, that this verse requires more than simply *understanding* Jesus' word or words. In fact Jesus' enemies often understood him fairly well. They understood on a previous occasion that he made himself equal with God. At the end of the present passage they apparently understand his claim to Deity, for they attempted to stone him. Had he merely claimed to be the Messiah, they would not have stoned him. They might have rejected and ridiculed him, but they did not equate a messianic claim with a claim to Deity. Others had made messianic claims without incurring such hatred. Later on the young man who was to become the Apostle Paul understood perfectly what the Christians were preaching: that is why he persecuted them. Clearly then Jesus in John 8:51 demands more than a simple understanding of his claim.

The "more" that goes beyond simple understanding is "keeping" his word. The verb "to keep" means: watch over, take care of, guard; give heed to, observe, notice, test by observation or trial; preserve, retain. From these connotations it follows that if some of the words or doctrines are commands, keeping means obedience. Other words, not commands, but doctrines such as the claims to be the Messiah, to be one with the Father, to be the Bread of Life and the Light of the world, are "kept" simply by believing them. Of course, no one can believe what he does not understand. Understanding is a prerequisite to belief, otherwise a missionary would not need to learn the native language.

Nevertheless the sole object Jesus refers to is his word, his words, his doctrine, dogma, or teaching. It is this that must be kept. Jesus does not speak of anything in addition to, hidden behind, or exalted above his doctrine. There is nothing irrational, mystical, illogical, or inexpressible to which he directs attention. The promise of escaping death is based completely and solely on Jesus' word: "if anyone kept my word, he shall never never see death ever."

Repetition may be tedious, but nevertheless kindly note again what John had said in a previous verse: "Ye seek to kill me because my doctrine makes no progress in you" (8:37). With this insistence on doctrine and word, it is positively amazing that even an Arminian can so misconstrue the Gospel of John and so attack those who believe John's words.

The sermon does not restrict itself to the Gospel of John, and to complete the argument we may follow it into I Corinthians. Dr. Tozer writes, "The theological rationalists say your faith should stand not in the wisdom of man but in the Word of God. Paul didn't say that at all. He said your faith should stand in the power of God. That's quite a different thing."

Is it? I do not think it can be quite a different thing. The antithesis between word and power is strained, for Dr. Tozer seems to have forgotten Luke 1:37, "No word from God is without power."[5] Remember also that the words are spirit and life (John 6:68). And though Dr. Tozer uses the epistle, he makes no mention of I Corinthians 1:24, where Christ, the *Logos*, is called the power of God as well as the wisdom of God. Power, wisdom, and word are identical, for in the simplicity of the divine essence all attributes merge. But let us see what Dr. Tozer says about I Corinthians 2:9-14.

It is the familiar passage, "Eye hath not seen, nor ear heard . . . the things of God knoweth no man, but the Spirit of God." To the end of verse 11, the author quotes in full, even the verse that says, "Unto us God revealed them through the Spirit." But verses 12-13 are omitted: "we received not the spirit of the world but the spirit which is from God that we might know the things that were freely given to us of God. Which things also we speak, not in words which man's wisdom teacheth, but which the Spirit teacheth, combining spiritual things with spiritual (words)." Then the author continues with verse 14. The impression that the author apparently wants to make, although he does not expressly draw the implication, is that knowledge of the truth is unimportant or even impossible. If this is not what he means, his quotation hangs in mid air: it does not connect with his immediately preceding antithesis between the power of God and the Word [capital W] of God. But when the passage is read in its entirety, one sees that this knowledge, unobtainable by scientific or empirical methods, is possible by revelation and was understood and believed by "us." The Apostle certainly distinguishes between two proposed methods of

---

[5] Any person who wants to empty the word of power must also have forgotten Hebrews 4:12, "The word of God is living and active, sharper than any two-edged sword." Some but not all ancient commentators took Hebrews to refer to Christ; but Protestants usually refer it to the Bible (cf. Calvin and Owen, *in loc.*). Reformed theologians sometimes accuse the Lutherans of so emphaizing the word of God that they render the Spirit superfluous. The Lutherans, of course, deny the charge; but true or not, the Lutherans could hardly have produced a doctrine subject to such a misunderstanding unless the Scripture itself had assigned great power to the word.

64

learning; but there is no disparagement of the truth nor any appeal to a "soul" that is different from the body of truths. The sermon does indeed contain several true and important statements. One is the author's insistence on the need of illumination. He says, "Revelation is not enough. There must be illumination before revelation can get into your soul." This is true. But the antithesis that the author draws between revelation and illumination is false. Illumination is not the "soul" of the truth. There is no implication that "the truth is *more* than the text." It is false to say that "there is something behind the text that you've got to get through to." Rather, illumination is what enables you to "get through" to the text. Illumination is a figure of speech, but it is not poetic nonsense. The figure compares light shining on a physical object with God's causing us to accept the truth. Note that it is the truth that God illumines. He does not substitute some other object beside, behind, or above the truth. Illumination does not alter, add to, or subtract from the truth. It causes us to focus on the truth just as it is. Thus, although the antithesis between experience and revelation is sound, the idea that illumination adds something to the truth and "gets us through to" some different object is unsound and false. If we want some poetry that is not nonsense, let us sing with Cowper, "The Spirit breathes upon the Word and brings the truth to sight."

The whole plan of salvation, so far as it is represented in this sermon, is unscriptural. It is substantially correct to say that "Conversion is a miraculous act of God by the Holy Ghost"; though it would be more accurately phrased as, Regeneration is a supernatural act of God, the Holy Spirit, for the Reformation in opposition to Romish superstition insisted that the age of miracles is past. Faith too is a supernatural gift of God. But the life which the new birth initiates and the faith that is its exercise is informed by the truth. It is not true to say, "God taught him in secret that truth had a soul as well as a body [this is poetic nonsense], and he dared to get through and pursue by penitence and obedience until God honored his faith and flashed the light on." Note how unbiblical this is. The human being "dares," "to get through" — whatever that means — and because of repentence and obedience, which are indubitably Scriptural requirements, God honors his faith and gives him illumination. This attributes merit to a man's daring. It obscures, really it denies that faith is a gift of God. Then because of this daring and faith, God rewards the man by giving him illumination. Preposterous! It is hard to get the plan of salvation more backwards than this. The Scripture nowhere teaches that faith is a reward of repentance and obedience. It is the free gift of God. One must first believe that what Christ says is true before he can repent and obey. Unless "the light is flashed on" at the beginning, a man will not accept the Scripture as truth.

Then, too, salvation includes sanctification as well as repentance, many other things, and finally glorification. Through the course of this life salvation is mostly the process of sanctification. Now, how is sanctification to be advanced? A few pages back, in the section on Truth, the verse was quoted, "Sanctify them by the truth: thy word is truth." Dr. Tozer's disparagement of truth and his substitution for it of something the Gospel never mentions would make sanctification, i.e., the whole Christian life, impossible. It is the truth, the word that sanctifies. Therefore the most important battle line is that between the acceptance and the rejection of God's truth. Everything else is subsidiary. Or, better, there is nothing else, for God's truth includes the doctrine of creation, the doctrine of the Atonement, and everything else. The Jews did not accept, they did not assent to the truth of God. To them Jesus said, "If anyone retains my *doctrine*, he shall never never see death ever."

Disparagement of doctrine, in our age, derives mainly from Soren Kierkegaard. Schleiermacher, the father of Modernism, may have lent some indirect help. When he replaced the word of revelation with religious experience, he undermined all Christian doctrine. But he did not mean to repudiate all doctrine. By a psychological analysis of religious experience he aimed to establish some principles of religion. He even thought that these principles would be Christian. But the history of the movement has demonstrated, as Feuerbach early saw, that the result is atheistic humanism. Yet humanism has dogmas too, not so eternally fixed and true as Christian doctrine, but, tentative though they may be, intellectual propositions concerning the values of life. It may possibly be that they think their empirical method eternally fixed and true and not merely tentative. But the values change. Some of Schleiermacher's disciples also, toward the end of the nineteenth century, especially in stressing Schleiermacher's Kantianism, decided that life's values could not be intellectually supported and therefore made religion a matter of the emotions. In this way they contributed to anti-intellectualism. But the most powerful and responsible source of anti-intellectualism, the one whose influence is so widespread today, is Soren Kierkegaard.

Many religious people who have never studied the history of philosophy, among them a number of devout but uninstructed Christians, are impressed with Kiekegaard's earnestness and zeal. When he speaks of passionate inwardness, he strikes in them a responsive chord. They echo Goethe's dictum that life is green and theory gray. They want excitement, not understanding. They want even less under-standing than Kierkegaard required.

Kierkegaard[6] required and insisted that a Christian must understand that orthodox theology is absurd. The Incarnation and the doctrine of the God-man, and by implication everything else, are not merely "above reason," they are precisely *against* reason — a phrase found at least a dozen times in the *Postscript*. Further reading will discover that Kierkegaard considers Christian doctrine as a violation of the laws of logic — identity, contradiction, and excluded middle. On pages 238-239 of the *Postscript* (tr. by Swenson and Lowrie, Princeton University Press, 1941) he repeats the problem of Abraham as an example, and on page 518 he says, "Sin is not a dogma or a doctrine for thinkers . . . it is an existence-determinant, and precisely one which cannot be thought." Three lines below he says that the paradox of Christianity "requires faith against the understanding." A few pages earlier (p. 513) he speaks of a contradiction that cannot be resolved and finds that the Incarnation is "contra-dictory to all thinking." Kierkegaard does indeed insist on understanding, for a Christian must understand that doctrine is irrational "in order to believe against understanding" (p. 503). "Faith requires a man to give up his reason . . . here again it appears how improper it is to transform Christianity into a doctrine to be understood" (p. 337). "Christianity is not a doctrine but an existential communication expressing an existential contradiction" (p. 339).

In opposition to Kierkegaard two things may be said. The first is a speculative remark, philosophical, theoretical, altogether intellectual, and absolutely conclusive. It is this: a writer who allows himself one contradiction cannot deny himself or anyone else another contradiction. Hence when Kierkegaard asserts that Christianity is not a doctrine, but an existential contradiction, one may reply: Yes, you are right, but since absurdity is permissible, Christianity is also a doc-trine and not an existential contradiction. More generally expressed: the assertion of a contradiction is absurd, non-sense, meaningless, and needs no other refutation.

The second thing to be said in opposition to Kierke-gaard is that his views are completely opposite to the Gospel of John, and are therefore anti-Christian. The evidence for this assertion is all the exposition found in the present study of the Gospel. But one point will make the matter utterly clear. Kierkegaard repeatedly says that it makes no difference *what* one believes: the important thing is *how* one believes it

---

[6] Or at least Johannes Climacus, in the *Concluding Unscientific Postscript*; for this is not the place to discuss the relationship between Kierkegaard and his pseudonyms.

(cf. p. 540). The crucial case is that of a Hindu idolater. "If one who lives in the midst of Christendom goes up to the house of God, the house of the true God, with a true conception of God in his knowledge, and prays, but prays in a false spirit;[7] and one who lives in an idolatrous community prays with the entire passion of the infinite, although his eyes rest upon the image of an idol: where is the most truth? The one prays in truth to God, though he worships an idol . . ." (pp. 179-180).

We object. If the Hindu worships in truth, then it is useless to command Christians to "Make disciples of all nations, teaching them to observe all things whatsoever I commanded you." And Jesus must have taught falsehood when he said, "No one comes to the Father but by me."

---

[7] Question: Is it possible to hold a true conception of God and pray in a false spirit? At any rate, the present writer's argument contains no defense of hypocrisy.

# Chapter 5

## SAVING FAITH

In view of the clear and repeated assertions of the Gospel it is strange that anyone who considers himself conservative or even orthodox should minimize faith or belief and try to substitute for it some emotional or mystic experience. Two possible explanations may be suggested. The first is that these people are so impressed by the spectacular conversion of the Apostle Paul that they think all conversions should conform to this type. Such a view cannot be rationally justified. In the first place the persecutor on his way to Damascus was not merely converted: Christ appeared unto him (making him a witness of the Resurrection) "to appoint thee a minister and a witness both of the things wherein thou hast seen me, and of the things wherein I will appear unto thee; delivering thee from the people, and from the Gentiles, unto whom I send thee, to open their eyes ..." (Acts 26:15-18). Such an appointment to apostleship should not be made the required type for every conversion. Indeed it is not the type even for every apostle. There were eleven others. Who appeals to their conversion experiences? Their conversion experiences are not recorded; and the various other conversions that are recorded differ from Paul's and from each other. It is therefore wrong to elevate anyone's experience to the level of a norm for everyone.

The second possible explanation of the strange disparagement of faith or belief is the romantic notion that sensory titillation is "experience" and sober logical thought is not "experience." Hence people who do not suffer ecstacies of joy or depths of despair are said to be devoid of Christian experience. But such a view has more in common with the pagan Goethe than with the Apostle John. It is likely that romanticism thrives on inborn tendencies plus an inability to think clearly, especially to think clearly about one's own (I shall not say experience) mental life. These people do indeed have beliefs. Many of them believe that the Bible is the Word of God and that Christ's death was a substitutionary sacrifice. But because they have studied so little, because their the-

69

ology is limited to a few fundamentals, and because they assume the detailed and onerous duties of pastors and evangelists where their limited theology is inadequate, they conclude from the meagreness of their thinking that thinking and believing are inadequate. Combined with this is their failure to notice the effect of their few beliefs on their own conduct.

As a man thinketh, so is he. Out of the heart — and as we shall see some pages farther on, *heart* means mind or intellect — are the issues of life. If a man says he has faith, but does not have works, we tend to conclude that he has no faith. Conduct, particularly habitual conduct, is the best criterion fallible men have for judging hypocrisy. What a man believes, really believes, even if he says the contrary, will show in his living. Therefore these popular evangelists show by their conduct that they believe some things. Their intellectual capital controls their actions so far as their capital reaches. But because they are under-capitalized, and because they have too little intellectual endowment to recognize how intellectual beliefs control them, they minimize theology and take refuge in romanticism.

In these introductory remarks to this chapter the meaning of the Scriptural term *heart* has been anticipated. Faith and belief have been emphasized. Even apart from these introductory inducements the nature of saving faith is an important division of theology. Therefore one should pay strict attention to what John's Gospel says on the subject.

Although John never uses the noun *faith (pistis)* in his Gospel, and only once in his epistles, he scatters its verb *(pisteuoo)* about in abundance — just about one hundred times. The main uses can be divided into two categories, depending on its object. The first object is a noun or pronoun governed by the preposition *in* (*eis* with the accusative or *en* with the dative). The second object is a clause. Sometimes also a noun occurs without a preposition, and there are instances when the object is unexpressed.

The usage with the noun-object seems to lend support to the liberal contention that Christians must believe in a Person, not a doctrine. God, they say, never reveals any thing, information, or doctrine: he reveals himself. Of course, modern theologians care little for the words of Scripture, and why they should accept the use of *pisteuoo* with a noun while rejecting many other things in Scripture is what they cannot explain. Nevertheless a conservative, an evangelical, one whose principle is *sola Scriptura*, must examine these words and this usage regardless of liberal oscillations.

From among the many instances of the noun-object the following are typical.

John 1:12; 2:23, 3:18 have the phrases "believed in his name" (*eis to onoma*). Comments on the usage will be

70

postponed until the list is ended; but one may note how Hebraic and non-hellenistic the reference to the name is. The phrase, "believed in him" is found in John 2:11; 3:15 (*en autooi*); 3:18; 4:39; 6:29 (*eis on*); 6:35 (*eis eme*); 6:40, on to 16:9 (*eis eme*). To "believe on the Son" occurs in John 3:36; 9:35; 12:11 (on Jesus). There are also instances where the noun or pronoun is a simple dative without a preposition. The pronoun is *me* in John 4:21, 5:46; 8:45-46; and 10:37. The pronoun *him* is in John 5:38 and 8:31. These listings are not complete or exhaustive, but they are typical and will serve the present purpose.

The present purpose is to show that these noun or pronoun objects are linguistic forms that simplify the text by implying without expressing the propositions to be believed. One of the clearest is John 4:21, "Woman, believe me." In this case the proposition to be believed follows explicitly: "Woman, believe me, that a time is coming when. . . ." There is no antithesis between believing Jesus as a person and believing what he says. Similarly John 5:46 compares believing Moses (dative without a preposition) and believing me. In both cases the object of belief is not a person without words, but definitely the words of the person. The *me* of John 8:45, 46 again refers to the truth I am saying. The "Do not believe me" of John 10:37 means, Do not believe what I say. The same explanation holds for 5:38 and 8:31. In both cases the reference is to an explicit *logos*.

The instances with the preposition *eis* are not always so obvious; but obviously they do not contradict what has just been said. For example, "to those who believe on his name" (1:12); "many believed on his name" (2:23); and "he has not believed on the name of the only Son of God" (3:18); all these with their Old Testament background imply that what is believed or not believed is the claim Jesus makes. If 2:23 can be closely connected with 2:22 (it is clearly the same place, the temple; and the time cannot be much later), the background is Psalm 69:9 and the words of Jesus himself. His act of cleansing the temple caused many to believe these propositions.

The second category of the uses of the verb *believe* has the propositional object explicit in the text. Without counting the cases where the object is clearly a proposition, although not explicitly given, a full 25 percent of the instances of *believe* have the proposition written out in full.

The first verse, already cited (2:22), does not itself contain the propositions believed: they are in the preceding context. The disciples believed Psalm 69:9 and the words Jesus had addressed to the Jews.

The second verse (3:12) also finds the explicit proposition in the context. Jesus said to Nicodemus, "If I have

71

spoken to you on earthly matters [such as the new birth and the Spirit's effect on men] and you do not believe, how will you believe (my propositions) if I speak of heavenly matters [such as the doctrine of the eternal generation of the Son and the inter-trinitarian relationships]?" The second set of propositions are of course not given; the first set constitutes the previous conversation explicitly reported.

The third verse (4:21), also previously cited, itself contains the proposition. John 4:41, 50 both have the noun-object *words* or *word;* but the propositions are explicit in the context. Similar are the two instances in 5:47, *viz.,* Moses' writings, not quoted, and Jesus' words contained in the preceding verses.

John 6:69 says, "We believe and know that thou art the Holy One of God." John 8:24 says, "You do not believe that I am [Jehovah, or, the one I claim to be]." John 9:18, "the Jews did not believe that he had been blind." John 10:25, 26, "I told you [that I am the Christ] and you do not believe [that proposition]; the works I do . . . testify of me [that I am the Messiah], but you do not believe [the propositions they assert]." John 11:26, 27, "Everyone who is alive and believes in me will never die. Do you believe this [proposition]? Yes, Lord, she said, I have believed that thou art the Messiah, the Son of God, who comes into the world." In John 11:42 Jesus spoke out loud "so that the crowd would believe that thou didst send me." But why tediously quote in addition 12:38, 47; 13:19; 14:10-11, 29; 16:27, 30; 17:8, 21; 19:35 and 20:31?

The conclusion is, not only that the verb *believe* (*pisteuoo*) may have a clause or proposition for an object, but that this is the fundamental meaning of the verb *believe.* In literary usage one may say that one believes a person; but this means that one believes what the person says. The immediate and proper object of belief or faith is a truth (or falsehood), a meaning, the intellectual content of some words; and this intellectual content is in logic called a proposition.

It may possibly be the case that the King James version has been a small factor contributing to anti-intellectualism. In German the Greek verb *pisteuoo* is translated *glauben,* and the noun is *der Glaube,* belief. Therefore Matthew 9:22 in German is, "*Tochter, dein Glaube hat dir geholfen.*" And Matthew 6:30 is, "*O ihr Kleingläubigen.*" But in English the connection between the Greek verb *believe* and its Latin noun is obscured by translating the noun as *faith* instead of *belief.* The Latin language has not been an unexceptionable advantage to theology. *Dikaiooo* was translated *justus-facere;* and thus the New Testament word for *acquit* or pronounce righteous was taken to mean *make righteous.* The result was a theory of infused grace that obscured the method of salvation until the time of Luther and the Reformation. So too it would have been better if the King James version had omitted the word *faith* and emphasized the root meaning of belief.

Because *fides* or faith permits, though it does not necessitate, a non-intellectual interpretation, the liberals today want us to have "faith" in a god who is unknowable and silent because he is impotent to give us any information to believe. This Latin anti-intellectualism, permitted by the noun *fides*, undermines all good news and makes Gospel information useless. Although the theologians of the sixteenth and seventeenth centuries would have repudiated twentieth century anti-intellectualism, their Latin heritage adversely affected some of their views. Before this earlier material is discussed, however, we must turn once again to the text in order to see precisely what is the effect of believing certain propositions.

This part of the study pays no attention to the grammatical object of the verb. Reliance is now placed on the conclusion already drawn that noun and pronoun objects are linguistic simplifications of the intended propositional object. To believe a person means precisely to believe what he says.

The first case, John 1:12, asserts that those who believe in his name have the right, graciously given by God, to be the children of God. The phrase "in his name," I take it, means his character as Messiah and Lord. Those who believe that Jesus is the Messiah prophesied in the Old Testament have the authority to be God's children.

The same idea occurs in John 3:15, 36. Everyone who believes in Jesus, believes that he is the Messiah, has eternal life. The converse is stated in verse 18. That the noun-object, or phrase *in his name*, bears this meaning is a little clearer in 5:24, where the person who hears Jesus' discourse (*logos*) and believes the Father, who sent him with the message, has eternal life and has (already) crossed over from death to life. To be sure, a random intellectual belief of an unregenerate man will not save him. The difficulty lies, not in belief as such, but in the fact that an unregenerate man is incapable of believing the necessary propositions. As John 12:30-40 says, "They could not believe because . . . he has blinded their eyes and hardened their hearts." If God had opened their eyes and had exchanged their heart of stone for a heart of flesh, they would have believed the Gospel message and so would already have passed from death to life. It is regeneration to eternal life that causes the intellectual belief. Thus acceptance of the propositions is a mark of having been regenerated and of having eternal life.

Again, John 6:40, 47, "Everyone who contemplates the

Son and believes on him has life eternal. . . . Most assuredly I tell you, the man who believes has eternal life." Similar phrases are found in 7:38; 8:31; and 11:25.

More explicit verses are the following. John 8:24 puts the matter negatively: "If you do not believe that I am [Jehovah, or, the Messiah] you will die in your sins." The force of this negative is important. The proposition "All believers have eternal life" does not imply that all non-believers lack eternal life. Such an implication would be invalid, as may be seen in an example from daily affairs: the proposition "all voters are residents" does not imply "all non-voters are non-residents." Therefore the simple statement "All believers are saved" allows the possibility that some unbelievers are saved as well. Belief may well guarantee eternal life; but without further information to the contrary something else may also guarantee eternal life. This elementary lesson in logic points up the importance of the explicit negative statement: if you do not believe, you will die in your sins. All believers are saved, and all the saved are believers.[1]

John 10:25-28 says, "You do not believe because you do not belong to my flock. My sheep listen to my voice. . . . I give them eternal life." This states what is essentially both the negative and the positive proposition; and the negative is clearly implied in 16:9, "He will convict the world of sin . . . because they do not believe on me." Then if one supposes that God granted the petitions of the high-priestly prayer, the positive statement is implied in 17:8-10, 16-17, 20-22, and 26.

Be sure to note that the Apostle John never mentions a mystic experience. He never says that one must get behind the text to something other than the words or doctrine. He repeatedly says, if you believe, you are saved. Belief is the whole thing. Indeed John in 20:31 asserts this very thing in stating the purpose for writing the Gospel: that you may believe the proposition that Jesus is the Messiah and that believing this proposition (and not in some other way) you may have life by his name.

The next question is, what does it mean to believe? This question is usually asked in Latin rather than in Greek, and so phrased the question becomes, What is faith? Various theologians have offered psychological analyses of faith. The most common Protestant analysis is that *fides* is a combination of *notitia*, *assensus*, and *fiducia*. If these last three Latin words can be explained, then one may compare *fides* and

---

[1] Jesus was speaking to adult Pharisees. The question of the salvation of infants is not here envisaged. Will not the mystics argue that since Jesus was speaking to Pharisees, his words do not apply to Gentiles today, who must do something other than believe?

*pistis* or *pisteuoo* to see if they are synonymous. If these Latin terms cannot be clearly defined, then they do not constitute an analysis of faith.

*Notitia* is not hard to define. The word refers to the intellectual content known. According to one large Latin lexicon *notitia* means *a being known, acquaintance* with a person (also sexual intercourse), *knowledge, conception, notion.* Examples would be the proposition that two and two are four, the realization that I must get my work done, the concept of *Liliaceae* in botany, and the doctrine of justification by faith. In specifying *notitia* as the first element in faith, the traditional Protestant analysis, whatever incipient anti-intellectualism may be buried in it, clearly intends to affirm that faith has an intellectual content.

Since some people understand the Gospel propositions — the Pharisees understood Jesus' claim better than the disciples did — but do not accept or believe them, *fides* must also contain acceptance or assent. Indeed *assensus*, one's voluntary acceptance of a proposition, seems to be more the essence of faith than anything else is. If we think of belief as believing, i.e., the subjective psychological activity, belief may be equated with assent. Objectively, belief, one's belief, is the *notitia*, the proposition believed. In the morning worship service, we recite our creed, our belief, our faith. Samuel Butler in *The Way of All Flesh* reports that the Anglican congregations in the eighteenth century recited The Belief, not The Creed. This belief is what the worshipper assents to. When the minister preaches the gospel, a person may understand what the speaker means; he may then assent to it; i.e., he believes. Instead of enumerating three elements in faith, one could better say that subjective belief, and assent are synonymous.

But then, apparently in opposition to Romanism, the Reformers wanted to say something else. In addition to believing, i.e., understanding and accepting, *fides* was said to include and require *fiducia*. What now is *fiducia*, this third element in saving faith?

The nature of saving faith and the difficulties of defining *fiducia* can be better appreciated by recalling some largely forgotten history. Luther and Calvin were not so clear on the matter as might be wished. Both of them in several places made assurance of salvation essential to faith. The implication is that unless one is certainly assured that God has saved him, he is not regenerate. Now, Luther's impetuosity led him many times to exaggerate his expressions: for example, his statement, Sin boldly! Luther also corrected his words, and there are passages in which he seems, at least seems, to deny that assurance is essential to saving faith. Calvin was much more cautious and careful than Luther. But

Calvin too seems, at least seems, to say that assurance is essential. But elsewhere he indicates that this is not really his opinion. It is possible that his unfortunate expressions came to mean something that he did not intend; for as time went on the later Lutheran and Reformed theologians gave more attention to assurance and developed distinctions that Calvin did not make. These developments took place after the first great controversies with the Roman church. Calvin's and Luther's chief attacks on Romanism centered on justification by faith. The nature of faith was indeed involved, but assurance was a minor issue; and the result was that they paid it insufficient attention. Nor is it the chief interest here. The subject is faith and *fiducia*. But if we examine the Reformers, earlier and later, the subject of assurance somewhat distorts the discussion.

Since the matter is of interest and importance, Calvin's own account will be given first. Calvin, *Institutes*, Book III, Chapter 2, has as its title "Faith Defined." The first paragraph is a transition from the preceding material and introduces the attempt to define faith by a reference to "the pernicious tendency of the mistakes of multitudes in the present age on this subject." Thus Calvin approaches his analysis with the contemporary situation in mind. Since he wrote before the Council of Trent, there is reasonable likelihood that the position he opposes is that of widespread common opinion rather than official Roman Catholic dogma. In view of this, and in view of Turretin, Le Blanc (who enumerate, as we shall see further on, several differences among the reformers), and the Westminister Confession, one may today wish to amend Calvin's remarks without any desire to detract from his great and amply deserved fame.

"A great part of the world," he continues, "when they hear the word *faith*, conceive it to be nothing more than a common assent to the evangelical history." He then distinguishes the "schools" from "a great part of the world." The souls (apparently) do a little better and identify God as the object of faith; but this too is inadequate. They should have specified Christ, for no man comes to God except by Christ.

The schools also (in paragraph 2) "have fabricated the notion of implicit faith, a term with which they have honored the grossest ignorance. . . . Is this faith — to understand nothing? . . . Faith consists not in ignorance, but in knowledge. . . . By this knowledge, I say, not by renouncing our understanding, we obtain entrance into the kingdom of heaven."

The intellectualism of this opening statement, so opposite to the worse than Romish ignorance of twentieth century liberalism, must be taken to govern the following exposition.

If Calvin denies that faith is one kind of knowledge, he must not be twisted to mean that faith is not knowledge.

Paragraph 3 continues, "Faith consists in a knowledge of God and Christ. . . . [the opponents, on the contrary] pretend that truth is held in error, light in darkness, and true knowledge in ignorance." In the following three paragraphs Calvin acknowledges that all Christians, even the apostles, are ignorant of some things, and that Christians normally and eventually learn more. Faith is indeed knowledge, but it is not omniscience.

In paragraph 7 Calvin explains why faith cannot simply be defined as a knowledge of God. Adam and Cain both knew God, but their knowledge terrified them. Hence faith requires a knowledge of God's mercy, not merely of God's law. Even so, if we know God's promises, yet if our knowledge is mixed with doubts, it is not faith. Faith is "uniform and steady," not "wavering and undecided." "Now, we shall have a complete definition of faith, if we say, that it is a steady and certain knowledge of the Divine benevolence toward us, which, being founded on the truth of the gratuitous promise in Christ, is both revealed to our minds and confirmed in our hearts by the Holy Spirit."

This definition and its preceding discussion are, in the main, excellent. They not only exploded the Romanism of their time, but they remain today superior to much of popular fundamentalism. There is, however, one point that needs criticism. Calvin seems to say that faith cannot be mixed with doubts; faith must be uniform and steady, not wavering and undecided. But this does not seem to square with John the Baptist's doubts when he was in prison. Nor do these phrases accord very well with the idea of faith as a grain of mustard seed, with the cry, Lord, I believe, help thou my unbelief, and with Christ's refusal to quench smoking flax. Calvin's definition seems to equate faith with assurance — something the later Calvinists did not do. However this may be, one thing is clear: Calvin's definition is not complete. The relationships between knowledge, which he stresses, and assent, which he will discuss a little later, and *fiducia*, if it be a third element, are not mentioned. This is not said to belittle Calvin, but to justify the researches of the later Calvinists.

In paragraph 8 Calvin attacks those who "maintain faith to be a mere assent, with which every despiser of God may receive as true whatever is contained in the Scripture." This statement is puzzling. It seems strange that a person who has received as true whatever is contained in Scripture could despise God. Does the Bible give any example of such a man? Did Simon Magus despise God? He placed a high value on the ability to confer the Holy Ghost by the laying on of hands.

No doubt selfish from one point of view, he nonetheless wanted this power, not for his own profit, but in order to give the Spirit to other people and so bless them. After being rebuked by Peter, he asked Peter to pray for him. Was this request insincere? At any rate, he could not have believed everything the Bible contains because he believed that apostolic gifts could be bought with silver. Nor does Calvin's next sentence provide him help for this puzzling statement. "But first," he continues, "it should be examined whether every man acquires faith for himself by his own power, or whether it is by faith that the Holy Spirit becomes the witness of adoption." The reference to adoption seems again to identify faith with assurance, and this is not the subject of discussion. Insofar as it implies that faith is a gift of God and is produced, not by the will of man, but by the Spirit's regenerating activity, well and good. But neither does this explain the nature and place of assent.

Embarrassing as it may be to the present writer in his aim of commending Calvin, the great Reformer actually says a few lines below (III, ii, 8), "The assent which we give to the Divine word . . . is from the heart rather than from the head, and from the affections rather than the understanding." But even here, it is still assent. When Calvin in his next phrase calls it "the obedience of faith," the word *obedience* warns us that assent is voluntary: it is an act of will, not of the affections. The will is active (activated by the Spirit, of course); affections as the name indicates are passive.

Even if in this section Calvin seems to disparage understanding, previous quotations show (I hope) his basic intellectualism. Here too he says, "Nothing is more precious to him [the Lord] than his own truth." Then he appends a remark that establishes assent: "As this is by no means a dubious point [the point that truth is precious to Lord], we conclude at once, that it is an absurdity to say that faith is formed by the addition of a pious affection to an assent of the mind; whereas even this assent consists in a pious affection." Though the present writer is not enamored of the word *affection*, for it denotes nothing voluntary, yet the result clearly makes faith an act of assent. That this act of assent is pious and caused by the Spirit is an emphasis with which the present writer agrees in Calvin's attack on any other view. The conclusion is that Calvin, perhaps not with perfect clarity, held that faith is assent.

Two nineteenth century theologians have written on this history. Robert L. Dabney, *Discussions: Evangelical and Theological*, Vol. I, in an examination of the aberrations of the Plymouth Brethren, goes over some of this Reformation history. His work should be consulted. But since his main subject is the Plymouth Brethren, it is better to spend a little space on the more directly pertinent article of William Cunningham, "The Reformers and the Doctrine of Assurance," in his *The Reformers and the Theology of the Reformation.* This thirty-eight page chapter is a gem. The present interest, however, is only to show that the term *fiducia*, which today is often confidently joined with knowledge and assent to make the definition of faith, has never been unambigously explained.

On page 122 Cunningham writes, "With respect to the nature of saving faith, the principal ground of controversy was this, that the Romanists held that it had its seat in the intellect, and was properly and fundamentally assent (*assensus*), while the Reformers in general maintained that it had its seat in the will, and was properly and essentially trust (*fiducia*). The great majority of eminent Protestant divines have adhered to the views of the Reformers upon this point, though some have taken the opposite side, and have held faith, properly so called, to be the mere assent of the understanding to truth propounded by God in his word. . . ."

Before another quotation is given, a small comment on the above should be made. The distinction between *assensus* and *fiducia* is here connected with a psychology that separates the intellect from the will. Probably a third faculty, either emotion (rarely considered by the Reformers) or sensibility, is joined to these to constitute the person. If this type of psychology is rejected and if more stress is put on the unitary person and his acts, it is at least possible that the analysis of faith will have to be altered. In the second place, in the history of theology, and even as far back as Stoic epistemology, assent was an act of will, not an act of intellect. Hence Cunningham has incorrectly reported Romanism and also makes a mistake in the psychological analysis.

More to the present point is the list of different meanings attached to the term *fiducia.* On page 130 Cunningham quotes Le Blanc, professor of theology at Sedan, as saying, "*fiduciam apud doctores Reformatos pluribus modis sumi . . .*" (trust is taken in several ways by the Reformed theologians). On the next page Le Blanc's words mean, "the Reformed theologians speak in various ways concerning fiducia; some say it is the primary part of faith; others deny this and hold that it is an effect of faith, but not properly essential to it; and others understand it one way and others another." Le Blanc then specifies four different meanings, of which Cunningham gives two. To these he adds three meanings specified by Turretin. A loose and incomplete translation is: *fiducia* is the assent or persuasion that arises from the practical judgment of the intellect concerning the truth and goodness of the gospel promises and concerning the power, will, and fidelity of the promising God. Second, *fiducia* is the

79

act of receiving Christ, by which the faithful Christian, when he has come to know the truth and goodness of the promises, flees to Christ, and embracing him, depends on his merit alone. Third, *fiducia* is the confidence or acquiescence and tranquillity which arises from the soul's taking refuge in Christ. Then Turretin adds, the first and second meanings are of the essence and definition of faith; but the third is only an effect and not part of the definition.

Cunningham concludes, "as these distinctions were not present to the minds of the Reformers, but were the growth of later speculations, we should not attribute to them any one of these distinct and definite opinions, without specific evidence bearing on the precise point to be proved, and should not allow ourselves to be carried away by the mere words, *trust* and *confidence*, *certainty* and *assurance*, without a full and deliberate consideration of the whole evidence bearing upon the meaning of the statements."

Before the Roman Catholic position is more definitely stated, a worse mistake than Cunningham's confusion will be given as an example of a common opinion. The Rev. Albert N. Martin, pastor of Trinity Church, North Caldwell, N.J., one of the best Puritan preachers of our day — and that means one of the best preachers of our day — in a pamphlet entitled, *What's Wrong with Preaching Today*, after making many wise and sobering remarks, says, "We must never forget . . . that faith was something more than an 'assensus,' a mere nodding of the head to the body of truth presented by the church as 'the faith.' . . . a mere nodding assent to the doctrines they are exposed to is not the essence of saving faith" (p. 18).

Mr. Martin is indubitably correct when he insists that "saving faith involved . . . a trust and commitment involving the whole man. . . ." But he seems to have misunderstood the nature of *assensus*. Assent is by no means "a mere nodding of the head." The Roman church may be a synagogue of Satan; the Pope may be the Anti-christ; but Roman Catholicism, which Mr. Martin contrasts with the Reformers on the point in question, never held what he says it held.

The *New Catholic Encyclopedia*, 1967, Vol. V, p. 798, in the article *Faith* says: "[The etymology of the word faith] points to an act of the intellect assenting at the command of the will for moral rather than severely intellection reasons. . . . Divine faith is fiducial assent to revealed truth . . . faith as such is an assent to truth . . . (p. 799) faith is the firm assent at the command of the will and under the inward motion of God's grace to the saving truths and supernatural mysteries God has revealed . . . (p. 800). St. Thomas . . . argued that in the act of divine faith there is a case of the will moving the mind to assent . . . that excludes all deliberate fear of being in error."

Although faith is so certain and is moreover "a gratuitous gift of God" (p. 804, *Loss of Faith*), a man may lose his faith because he can lose sanctifying grace. "Grace requires a man's free cooperation. This free cooperation can be withheld."

The second paragraph from the Catholic Encyclopedia denies the Reformation doctrine of the perseverance of the saints. It reduces the power of God to a dependence on man's cooperation. This is, of course, utterly unscriptural. But the first paragraph in analyzing faith even uses the word *fiducia* in the phrase "fiducial assent to revealed truth." Apparently Romanism holds that *fiducia* instead of being a third independent element in faith is a characteristic of assent. But it shows how wrong certain Protestants are when they identify assent with a mere nodding of the head. Since such mistakes are made in reporting Romanism — which ought to be a reasonably easy matter — it is possible that the more difficult psychological analysis may also be imperfect.

It has already been established that Protestant theologians have proposed several different analyses. Le Blanc noted the fact and specified four possibilities. Then he added three others from Turretin, one of which identifies *fiducia* and *assensus;* and this definition Turretin considers the essence of faith, while the third is not part of the definition.

The question now is, Can *fiducia* be so defined as to make it an independent third element in faith, or is faith essentially assent to a known proposition?

The Puritan writer Thomas Manton in his excellent commentary on the epistle of James gives a characteristic and significant answer. The paragraph in question discusses James 2:19, "The devils also believe and tremble." "This instance showeth," says Manton, "what faith he disputeth against; namely, such as consisteth in bare speculation and knowledge. . . . *Thou believest,* that is, assentest to this truth; the lowest act of faith is invested with the name of believing."

Manton's argument here is that since the devils assent and true believers also assent, something other than assent is needed for saving faith. This is a logical blunder. The text says the devils believe in monotheism. Why cannot the difference between the devils and Christians be the different propositions believed, rather than a psychological element in belief? Manton assumes a different psychology is needed. It is better to say a different object of belief is needed.

According to Manton the devils' psychology is one of bare speculation. However, he does not explain what this is. If it is the so-called faith, discussed on his preceding pages,

81

that produces no works, one cannot object. This so-called faith Manton calls a "dead faith," or better a "false faith," and therefore not a saving faith at all. Faith without works is dead. Agreed. But if this is not saving faith at all, and is yet called faith and belief, the difference will be found in the object, not in the psychological analysis. The analysis is the same whether a person believes a saving truth, a non-saving truth, or even a falsehood.

Manton makes an attempt to avoid the force of this consideration. "There is one God," he continues. "He instanceth in this proposition, though he doth limit the matter only to this: partly because this was the first article of the creed . . . by it intending also assent to other articles of religion. . . ."

Now, just what devils believe and do not believe, the Bible does not fully explain. The psychology of Satan is something of a puzzle. Apparently Satan really believed that Job would curse God. Like the Arminians he did not believe in the perseverance of the saints. One cannot be certain, but possibly Satan believed the promise he himself made to Eve. Did he not also believe that he might possibly tempt Christ to sin? If he had believed it impossible, why should he have tried three times? There must therefore be a good bit of the Bible that the devils do not believe.

In this difficulty it is best to stay close to the text, and James says only that the devils believe there is one God. The text nowhere says that this proposition stands for all the articles of the creed. It has just now been proved that it does not. If human beings can be monotheists without believing in the Atonement, or even in Christ, one might suppose the devils could too. Because Manton adds to the creed of the devils propositions James does not specify, his argument becomes confused. Depending on an hypothesis that has no textual foundation, he fails to escape the objection above: it is illogical to conclude that belief is not assent just because belief in monotheism does not save. The clearer inference is that if belief in monotheism does not save, then one ought to believe something else in addition. Not assent, but monotheism is inadequate.

Manton definitely asserts, "The devils also believe: That is, assent to this truth, and other truths revealed in the word." Of course, they do: they believe that Eve yielded to their temptation; no doubt they believe that Moses led the Israelites out of Egypt. But to suggest that they believe all other truths revealed in the word goes beyond James' text, and contradicts other parts of the Scripture.

Manton continues. "Bare assent to the articles of religion doth not infer true faith." Here the weasel word is "bare." Does he mean a mere nodding of the head? Probably not, for the devil's belief or assent is more than that. It is difficult to guess what Manton's psychology of "bare" assent is. The truth that saving faith produces works does not advance the argument. To say that true or saving faith (since belief in a falsehood is true or genuine belief) produces works does not imply that faith is other than assent. Why should not assent produce works? It produced trembling. But if "bare" assent is not identified with assent minus works, then Manton assigns no meaning to the word on which he so much depends.

We agree that "True faith uniteth to Christ, it is conversant about his person." But we question "It is not only *assensus axiomati*, an assent to a Gospel maxim or proposition; you are not justified by that, but by being one with Christ." But is it not assent to the Gospel that makes a man one with Christ? What is meant by "being one with Christ?" Manton operates on the mistaken philosophical view, prevalent among contemporary dialectical theologians, that there are two kinds of knowledge. He admits that the Reformers did not accept this philosophy: "It was the mistake of the former age to make the promise, rather than the person of Christ, to be the formal object of faith." But this was not a mistake. The earlier Reformers and the later Scottish Presbyterians had the right idea. There is no divorce between Christ's words and himself. Christ's *logoi* and *rheemata* are Christ's mind, and Christ's mind is himself. The detailed study of John's Gospel, traced carefully in the previous chapters, shows the apostolic emphasis on words and argument. There is no theory of two kinds of knowledge.

But if assent is not enough, as Manton argues, what else is needed? Do these people who disparage belief in opposition to John have anything definite to add? If they cannot specify and identify the addition they have in mind, they have no addition in their minds, and their contention falls. Here now is the explanation Manton offers.

"In short, there is not only assent in faith, but consent; not only an assent to the truth of the word, but consent to take Christ.[1] There must be an act that is directly and formerly [formally?] conversant about the person of Christ. Well, then, do not mistake a naked illumination[2] or some general acknowledgment of the articles of religion for faith. A man may be right in opinion and judgment, but of vile affections; and a carnal Christian is in as great danger as a pagan or idolater or heretic;[3] for though his judgment be sound, yet his manners are heterodox and heretical. True believing is not an act of the understanding only, but a work of the heart (Acts 8:37).[4] I confess some expressions of Scripture seem to lay much upon assent, as I John 4:2, and 5:1; I Corinthians 12:3; Matthew 16:17; but these places do either show, that assents, where they are serious and upon full conviction, come from some special revelation;[5] or else, if they propound them as evidences of grace, we must distinguish times. The greatest difficulty then lay upon assent, rather than affiance. The truths of God suffering under so many prejudices, the Gospel was a novel doctrine, contrary to the ordinary and received principles of reason, persecuted in the world, no friend to natural and carnal affections, and therefore apt to be suspected. The wind that bloweth at our backs, blew in their faces; and that which draweth on many to assent to the Gospel was their discouragement. Consent and long prescription of time, the countenance and favor of the world, do beget a veneration and reverence to religion; and therefore assent now is nothing so much as it was then, especially when it is trivial and arreptitious [demonic or raving], rather than deliberate: for this is only the fruit of human testimony, and needeth not supernatural grace.[6] Therefore do not please yourselves in naked assents; these cost nothing, and are worth nothing. There is a form of knowledge (Rom. 2:2), as well as a form of godliness (II Tim. 3:3). A form of knowledge is nothing but an idea or module of truth in the brains, when there is no power of virtue to change and transform the heart."

Manton's argument is typical of and fuller than most of those that aim to add a third element to *notitia* and *assensus*. In spite of its length it has been given in full to assure the reader that nothing of importance has been omitted. Criticism will show that certain of its propositions are indubitably true, but that a few unscriptural assertions and considerable confusion make the whole a logical fallacy. Since the points are numerous, it seems best to frame the criticism after the manner of footnotes, numbering each in sequence so as to make it easy to follow.

1. The psychological element that Manton wishes to add to knowledge and assent in order to constitute faith is *consent*. This is his conclusion, stated first; and the remainder of the quotation is his argument to support the conclusion. If the word *consent* has a definite meaning different from knowledge and assent, and if his argument is valid, Manton will have proved his point. But if he fails in either of these two requirements, he fails *in toto*.

2. It is interesting to note that Manton minimizes illumination, while this was what Dr. Tozer considered to be the all important element. Of course, Dr. Tozer misunderstood the Reformed meaning of illumination, and what Manton thinks "naked" illumination is, is not clear. One of Manton's unpleasant habits is that of attaching obfuscating adjectives to important nouns. When the Bible talks about illumination, even if the word itself is not used, it refers to the power of

the Holy Ghost as he causes a man to understand and accept the truth. If the adjective "naked" is attached, it probably means, since neither Manton nor Dr. Tozer want to deny that man himself is present, that truth and revelation are not present. But with this understanding of Manton's word "naked," his argument applies to nothing at all. Scriptural illumination always focuses the mind on the message.

3. That a carnal Christian is in as great danger as a pagan is unscriptural. No one is to be commended for his carnality. Paul berated the carnal Christians in Corinth. But though their works shall be burned up, yet they themselves shall be saved. The carnal Christian is even somewhat better off than this. Since justification inevitably produces sanctification, the most depraved sinner who is born again must improve, perhaps slowly and with much difficulty, or sometimes with the success of John Newton. The pagan is in danger of hell fire; the carnal Christian is not. To the extent that Manton depends on this false premise, to that extent his argument is vitiated.

4. Here Manton falls into a great, though common, confusion. The trouble is not that Acts 8:37 is spurious. None of the earliest and best manuscripts have it. But there are many other verses that insist one must believe with the heart: e.g., "If thou shalt confess with thy mouth . . . and believe in thy heart . . ." (Rom. 10:9-10). Rather the trouble is that Manton has failed to understand what the Bible means by the term *heart*. He wrote, "True believing is not an act of the understanding only [and he really means, not of the understanding and of the will together], but a work of the heart." For him therefore the heart is something other than the understanding. But in the Bible the *heart*, in about 70 or 75 percent of the instances, means the understanding, without affirming or denying the presence of a volition. In another 20 percent, approximately, the term *heart* means the will, with or without an explicit reference to the understanding. Accordingly less than 10 percent of the instances refer to anything other than intellect and will. Manton's spurious verse itself says that the heart believes. Now, belief is definitely intellectual and volitional. The good news, i.e., information, must be understood and assented to. This is belief; and it is the *heart* that believes. Therefore the heart is the intellect.

Some other verses that show the intellectual nature of the heart now follow, but the reader is urged to check through a concordance and examine all the occurrences of the term.

Genesis 6:5. "Every imagination of the thoughts of his heart was only evil continually."

Genesis 8:21. "Jehovah said in his heart, I will not again. . . ."

Genesis 17:17. "Then Abraham . . . said in his heart, shall a child be born. . . ."

Genesis 20:6. "In the integrity of thy heart thou hast done this."

I Samuel 2:35. "A faithful priest that shall do according to that which is in my heart and in my mind."

Psalm 4:4. "Commune with your own heart."

Psalm 12:2. "They speak falsehood . . . and with a double heart do they speak."

Psalm 14:1. "The fool hath said in his heart, There is no God."

Psalm 15:2. "He . . . speaketh truth in his heart."

Isaiah 6:10. "Lest they . . . understand with their heart."

Isaiah 10:7. "Neither doth his heart think so."

Isaiah 44:18, 19. "He hath shut . . . their hearts that they cannot understand. And none calleth to mind [the same word, heart] neither is there knowledge nor understanding."

A moderately careful study of these verses will show that the heart is the organ of understanding and knowledge. It is the heart that thinks. When any popular preacher contrasts the head and the heart, meaning that the heart is something other than the intellect, he is distorting Scripture and thinks falsehoods in his heart. Since this particular misunderstanding of Scripture is uniformly a part of the argument against identifying faith or belief with assent, these verses and many others constitute a complete refutation.

5. The Scripture is so clear that believing is volitional assent to an understood proposition that Manton cannot avoid paying some attention to a few such references. He lists I John 4:2 and 5:1, also I Corinthians 12:3, and Matthew 16:17. He could have added Romans 10:9-10 and many other verses in the Gospel of John. Manton tries to escape the plain force of these verses by arguing that "assents, where they are serious and upon full conviction come from some special revelation." This quotation contains both error and confusion. It is confused because it seems to presuppose that some acts of assent are not "serious." Every act of assent is serious or honest, since assent is never a mere nodding of the head. But though honest, it does not have to be with "full conviction." According to Manton's words the only person who could assent with full conviction would be a recipient of a special revelation, i.e., a prophet or an apostle. Now, some people may assent with full conviction or assurance of salvation. I John 5:1, which Manton cites, speaks of "Whosoever believeth . . ." not just an apostle. Of course, the apostles, who received the message directly from God assented upon

full conviction. Others do too. But still others do not. There are people with little faith, like a grain of mustard seed. Thus Manton's argument is both confused and contains error. It therefore breaks in pieces on the rock of Scripture.

6. He has, however, given himself another hatch of escape: if assent is taken as evidence of grace, and not of a prerogative of an apostle only, then "we must distinguish the times." Now, at the beginning, it would seem that if assent was saving faith in the first century, the plan of salvation has not so changed that assent is no longer saving faith in the seventeenth and twentieth centuries. One cannot accept the proposition that what saved then no longer saves now. Of course, it is true that the gospel was a strange, novel, and alien message in pagan Rome. It was a well-known and favorably-regarded message in seventeenth century England. Therefore one may agree that there were fewer hypocrites in Rome than in England. But then Manton tries to denigrate full conviction by joining to it what is "trivial and arreptitious." Obviously, therefore, his argument is a fallacy. Assent still needs "supernatural grace." And as the work of the Holy Spirit's irresistible grace, it is saving faith. Manton then reasserts "naked assents" (which are not assents), and compares them with "a form of knowledge" (that is not knowledge). All this is irrelevant.

What is relevant and what was necessary he has omitted: a precise definition of "consent" that would clearly distinguish it from both *notitia* and *assensus*. Astonishing as it may seem, Manton never even tried to define "consent." Without its being arreptitious, consent remains a naked and trivial word without meaning. Saving faith remains an intellectual assent — not to any random proposition, such as "there is one God," but to the doctrine of the Atonement.

The desire to find a third element in faith, in addition to understanding and assent, seems, if we may judge by popular preaching, to be aided by a psychological illusion. Preachers often use an illustration such as this: You may believe that a bank is sound by having read its financial statement, but you do not and cannot trust it until you deposit your money there. Making the deposit is faith. So, these preachers conclude, belief in Christ is not enough, no matter how much you read the Bible and believe that it is true. In addition to believing you must also trust Christ. That is faith.

The psychological illusion arises from the fact that the two cases are not parallel. In the case of the bank, there is the factor of depositing money. I have some dollar bills to be deposited; I go and deposit them in Bank X and not in Bank Y. Therefore I trust Bank X and do not trust Bank Y. But such is not the case. The reason I deposit money in this bank and not another is simply that my financial condition is far from warranting two bank accounts. I believe that Bank Y is quite as sound as Bank X. Both have competent administrators. Then too they both insure all depositors up to $10,000.00, and my account is less than one tenth of this. I choose Bank X, not because I trust it more, but simply because it is nearer my home. This is a matter of convenience — not of faith. What is more, in the bank illustration there is a physical factor — depositing bills or checks; whereas in saving faith there is no such factor. Thus arises the illusion. Those who use such illustrations import into a spiritual situation something, a physical motion, that cannot be imported into it. There is nothing in the spiritual situation analogous to depositing the currency. There is believing only: nothing but the internal mental act itself. To suppose that there is, is both a materialistic confusion and an inadmissible alteration of the Scriptural requirement.

What better conclusion can there be other than the express statements of the Bible? Permit just one outside of John. Romans 10:9-10 says, "If you confess with your mouth that Jesus is Lord and believe in your mind that God raised him from the dead, you shall be saved." There is no mystical getting behind, under, or above the text; the only consent there is, is belief in the propositions. Believe these, with understanding, and you shall be saved. Anyone who says otherwise contradicts the repeated *rheemata* of Scripture.

Certainly John agrees with Paul and repeats Paul's idea: "Whoever believes in the Son has eternal life" (3:15, 36). "The believer has eternal life" (6:40, 47). "If anyone keeps my doctrine, he shall not see death ever" (8:51), and conversely, "He who does not receive (or grasp; cf. John 1:5) my words (rheemata) . . . that word (*logos*) which I have spoken will judge him in the last day" (John 12:48).


CONCLUSION. One reason, in my opinion, why popular evangelicalism, even though it professes the formal principle of *sola Scriptura* (and no one can call himself an evangelical in the traditional sense of the word unless he believes that Scripture is inerrant), stumbles at the view here derived from John's Gospel is its ignorance of the history of Christian doctrine. When a young person is brought up under a certain type of instruction, as for example Darby's dispensationalism, the person so brought up, even though the doctrine is only one generation old and had never before appeared in Protestantism, tends to think that it is standard orthodoxy. Conversely an old doctrine, forgotten, or, better, never learned by contemporaries, is looked upon as a new heresy. To combat this condition, Calvin was quoted; and Cunningham gave some account of several Reformed analyses of faith. But the doctrine of assent is far older than Calvin. Augustine in his *De Praedestinatione Sanctorum* (2,5) says, "To believe is to think with assent." The present monograph therefore proposes no new heresy, but defends an old established orthodoxy.

Another reason for contemporary reluctance to accept the Scriptural view of the "heart" or mind, and the role of faith or belief in salvation is the influence of romanticism and the anti-intellectualism of the reaction against Hegel. This is aided by the post-kantian emphasis on experience and the substitution of psychological analyses of feeling in place of revealed truth.

Those who have never studied philosophy and know nothing about the history of ideas absorb many of their opinions, unconsciously and at random, from the environing social climate. Unaware that their minds are being formed by the philosophic debris of a previous century, they unthinkingly consider their own views as Christian. One trained in philosophy knows the sources of his ideas. If he adopts some, he recognizes what he is doing. For example, Thomas Aquinas rejected Augustinianism and adopted Aristotelianism. He did so consciously, in opposition to the prevailing philosophy, because he thought that Aristotle could provide a better philosophic basis for Christianity than Augustine could. Since his procedure was deliberate and not at random, his results were fairly consistent. The mind of the uneducated man is full of contradictions. Thus it is that popular evangelicalism can profess *sola Scriptura* and have a doctrine of truth that borrows too much from Schleiermacher and Goethe.

The argument or *logos* of the present book, however, has paid only minimum attention to philosophy and the history of doctrine. It appeals directly to Scripture. And although the material comes almost exclusively from the Gospel of John, with only a few references from other books of the Bible, every objection to the doctrine of *logos*, or truth, or saving faith has been met or at least touched upon. Misunderstandings arise only because minds saturated with opposing views fail to give proper weight to what they read.

Understanding and assent are particularly objectionable to those who have romantic ideas of life. One devout and zealous Christian friend wrote that God is Will as well as Mind. Presumably his thought was that if man is made in God's image and man is mind only, God can have no will. Since, however, the view here defended has repeatedly stressed assent as an act of intelligent will, it seems strange that any reader would conclude that Mind and Will are two separate things. This person also insisted that life, Christian life, is not assent only, but also a life of hope, "new hope for the present and expectation for the future." But what is hope other than assent to and belief in certain propositions? Hope is the belief that God will receive me on the judgment day through the merits of Christ. Hope therefore is assent.

It has also been objected that assent does not produce life and that we trust a person with the heart rather than believe the truth with the head; and that experience should be decisive.

These matters have all been covered. Perhaps one point should be repeated. Assent is not the cause of eternal life. Nothing in this monograph says that it is. Assent, instead of being the cause, is the result of the Spirit's regenerating activity. The unregenerate mind is enmity against God. People do not believe because they are not part of the chosen flock; they cannot believe because God has blinded their eyes. Therefore regeneration must, absolutely must precede assent. For this reason assent or belief is the life that the Spirit gives. "He who hears my word and believes him who sent me . . . has passed from death to life" (5:24). The verb is in the perfect tense. A dead man can neither will nor believe; therefore God must first regenerate a man and give him the life that is necessary to voluntary assent.

This life of faith is a life of sanctification. Sanctification is a work of God's grace by which he renews his image in the regenerated subject. This process of sanctification takes place basically through an increase of knowledge (cf. II Peter 1:3 ff.). John very pointedly said, "The words I have spoken to you are spirit and life (6:68); and "You are already clean because of the theology I have spoken to you" (15:3); and "Sanctify them by thy truth; thy word is truth" (17:17). Hence it is that knowledge of and assent to the Bible that advances the Christian life.

This last verse points to the reason for it all and indicates the necessary connection between the *Logos*-doctrine and the doctrine of saving faith. John 17:17 shows that the Bible is truth. Because Jesus is the *Logos*, he was full of truth; truth arose or came into being through Jesus Christ. In fact, Jesus is the truth — the truth that is the way and the life as well. Behind all this stands the principle that God is Truth, and they that worship him must worship him in spirit and in truth.

Men are rational or intellectual beings because God created them in his image. To contemn truth and to embrace the irrationalities of mystic theology — which cannot in truth be *theo-logia* at all — is to contemn God. Conversely, if anyone guards my doctrine,

$$\theta\acute{\alpha}\nu\alpha\tau o\nu\ o\mathring{\upsilon}\ \mu\acute{\eta}\ \theta\epsilon\omega\rho\acute{\eta}\sigma\eta\ \mathring{\epsilon}\iota\varsigma\ \tau\grave{o}\nu\ a\mathring{\iota}\grave{\omega}\nu a\ !$$